ollins

Policy
MIDDLE STAGE

Enhanced English Alive Coursebook 6

Ruby Bose
Safa Abdul Razak
Series Editor
Renu Viswanath

Acknowledgements

The publishers wish to thank and acknowledge the following for granting us permission to use copyright material:

Todd-Michael St Pierre for *Cypress Street*. Reprinted with the permission of the author; Sarah Ismail for *I Speak Sign Language*. Reprinted with the permission of the author.

The publishers have applied for permission for the following:
Operation Blackbeard by Aabid Surti, *Travelling with Grandfather's Zoo* by Ruskin Bond, *Upon the Songs of Whales* by Cori MacNaughton; *Fight, Manju, Fight!* by Sigrun Srivastav, *Powerful Moves* by T. V. Padma, *The Tree House* by Sivakami Velliangiri, *Children at Work* by Gita Wolf and Anushka Ravishankar. Acknowledgements for these texts will be made in the future editions of the book.

Every effort has been made to trace copyright holders and to obtain their permission for the use of copyright material. However, in some instances, we have been unable to trace the owners of the copyright pieces published here. The authors and publishers will gladly receive any information enabling them to rectify any error or omission in subsequent editions.

Illustrations

Cover and Title Page: Created by Toonfantasy

Inside: Page 14: Ekolara, Trifonenko, Luplupme, Multipedia, Hennadii, Ekolara; **26:** Grafico2013, Jameslee1; **46–47:** Bkgd Exxorian; **47:** Turk Stock Photographer; **48** Emranashraf; **65–66** Nadzeya_Dzivakova; **70** Skathi; **100:** Targovcom, Imtmphoto, LOSHADENOK, Castenoid, Romrodinka, SerrNovik; **113:** MicrovOne; **115:** Michael Burrell, Gam1983, Mongpro, Prapann, Phanasitti, Janine Lamontagne, MoreenBlackthorne, Subodhsathe, Hadynyah, Anandoart; **119:** JodiJacobson; **137:** Man As Thep; **140:** Ananaline, Typhoonski, Labsas; **114:** Narakorn, Leontura; **151:** Exxorian, DimaChe. **86:** Wikimedia; **88:** Wikimedia; **117:** Sai Avinash/ Wikimedia; **140:** Wikimedia, Wikimedia.

Preface

Enhanced English Alive is a multi-skill course in English that adheres to the guidelines laid down by the **National Education Policy, 2020**. This edition retains the original essence of teaching communicative English using a cross-curricular approach and interactive and experiential teaching and learning methods. It offers high-quality English language materials with a coherent structured approach, effective integration of subject knowledge and life skills.

The series comprises Coursebooks and Workbooks for Foundational Stage (Nursery, LKG, UKG, Classes 1 and 2), Preparatory Stage (Classes 3 to 5), and Middle Stage (Classes 6 to 8). Literature Readers are for the Preparatory and Middle Stages (Classes 3 to 8). Each grade package includes a Teacher's Resource Pack and a Collins DigiSuite.

This series integrates the essence of **NIPUN Bharat** guidelines, which extensively deal with foundational literacy and numeracy. Each book aims to motivate learners to read independently, to improve their vocabulary, to develop their critical thinking and creative skills, as well as to enhance their ability to express themselves both verbally and in writing.

This series takes care of the requirements of **Structured Assessments For Analyzing Learning (SAFAL)**. Research-based activities and projects have been used to instill inquiry-based learning, while comprehension passages have been followed by extrapolative and value-based questions that involve analysis-based learning. Additionally, in the Middle Stage (Classes 6 to 8), an end-of-year Assessment Paper has been provided.

Key features

Coursebooks

- **Warm-up:** A wide variety of picture-based thematic activities and probing questions at the beginning of units initiate the learner into the subject and ensure his/her active engagement in the lesson. For grades 1 to 5, these activities are introspective and meditative inquiries that are based on the pedagogy of mindfulness as delineated in the NEP, 2020.
- **Reading:** Each book has well-chosen selections from a wide range of literary genres that are also useful in cross-curricular teaching. These include picture stories and comic strips.
- **Cross-curricular boxes:** This series specially covers topics that are interrelated with other subjects taught in the same grade. Dedicated boxes teaching these cross-curricular concepts are placed along the main text.
- **Glossary:** All new words in the text are highlighted and their meanings are given in simple language using the easiest possible words. Literary devices are also taught along with a glossary of literary terms.
- **Summary:** A short summary at the end of each text is provided for an easy way to remember the essence of the text.
- **Comprehension:** This section includes plenty of exercises including factual, inferential, and extrapolative questions.
- **Life Skills and Values:** There is a separate thematic section on life skills and values aimed at developing good character in students and equipping them with skills needed to cope with

different challenges in life. Guidelines set by NEP, 2020 have been followed in selecting these life skills and values.

- **Vocabulary:** Each chapter has boxed explanations of new vocabulary words and topics followed by a variety of exercises. Spelling is also taught in this section with proper rules and explanations. Moreover, dictionary skills are taught in books 3 to 8.
- **Grammar:** Grade-appropriate grammar is explained with several visual models and extensive examples from the learner's immediate world. Plenty of varied exercises follow them to ensure the learner has learnt the concept well.
- **Listening and Speaking:** This section aims at developing students' listening, speaking, and overall communicative skills through a wide variety of tasks and pair/group activities. Pronunciation is also covered in this section in books 3 to 8.
- **Writing:** This well-graded section has a variety of age-appropriate creative and scaffolded writing tasks. These cover informal and formal letters, diary entries, flow charts, posters, stories, biographies, notices, reports, travelogues, character sketches, book reviews, recipes, acrostic poems, articles, and picture-based compositions.
- **Activities:** There is a fun activity accompanying each poem. Most of these activities require working collaboratively in groups or pairs. These activities are varied and cover various twenty-first century life skills.
- **Projects:** Three well-designed cross-curricular projects are provided that are linked to topics taught in that particular grade in other subjects.
- **Assessment Paper:** A test paper is provided at the end of books 6 to 8 to assess the end-of-year preparation and comprehension skills of the learners.

Workbooks

The Workbooks have been carefully mapped to the Coursebooks, and created with the intention of independent learning. Each Workbook has 8 comprehension passages including poems. The vocabulary and grammar sections include a quick recap of the concepts covered in the corresponding chapter of the Coursebook. The listening, speaking, and writing sections allow learners extra practice. Additional assessment papers included in the Workbooks are patterned on the Structured Assessments For Analyzing Learning (SAFAL). These offer a scope for assessing the competencies of critical thinking, inquiry-based learning, and analysis-based learning.

Literature Readers

The Literature Readers teach critical appreciation of literature through short stories, folktales, fairytales, poems and extracts from classics from the literature of different ages. A summary at the end offers a revision and understanding of the essence of the text. Literary devices are also taught along with a glossary of literary terms.

Teacher's Resource Pack

The Teacher's Resource Pack contains model lesson plans, additional worksheets, and grammar-based projects covering all the pedagogical aspects included in the Coursebooks, along with listening texts and answer keys to all exercises across Coursebooks, Workbooks, Literature Readers, and additional assessment papers.

Key to Icons

Enhanced English Alive is a multi-skill course that is closely aligned with the National Education Policy, 2020. It uses an interactive approach, cross-curricular themes, and experiential activities to build communicative competence in students. This series aims to prepare learners with the various skills outlined in the National Education Policy, 2020. These skills have been tagged appropriately with easily recognizable icons for the user's convenience. Here is the key to all the icons used in this series.

Cross-Curricular Content

- The cross-curricular approach to a topic recognizes that all subjects are inter-linked. It includes contributions from several different disciplines or viewpoints for effective learning.
- All chapters have dedicated boxes teaching cross-curricular content appropriate to that class. These boxes cover the following:

  Science Scan covers topics related to science.

  Maths Magic covers topics related to mathematics.

  Earth Speak covers topics related to geography and environmental studies.

  Looking Back covers topics related to historical events and personalities.

  Fact File covers topics related to general knowledge and awareness.

  Lit Bits covers topics related to literature and famous literary figures.

  Art and Culture covers topics related to art and culture.

Twenty-First Century Skills

- The twenty-first century skills ensure that today's students can thrive in an ever-changing world and can use these skills to learn constantly.
- Here are the most commonly cited twenty-first century skills in this series:

Critical Thinking — Critical Thinking

Communication — Communication Skills

Collaboration — Collaboration

Creative Thinking — Creativity

ICT — Information Communication Technology Skills or Digital Literacy

Experiential Learning

- Experiential learning is a process of learning through hands-on experience. Here, students 'learn by doing' an activity followed by reflective observation on the experience from multiple perspectives.
- This method helps learners link existing knowledge to understand new concepts and apply it to make decisions.

Art Integration

- Art Integrated Learning (AIL) is a teaching-learning model that integrates fine arts (painting, sculpture, architecture, music, and poetry), performing arts (theatre and dance), and photography with teaching new concepts.
- This provides students with an experiential and a multi-disciplinary learning experience.

Happiness Content

- Learning should be an enjoyable process for learners. It should focus on building and understanding new concepts rather than rote learning.
- Children should experience happiness through learning and awareness, active participation in class, and also in their relationships with their friends and family.

India Focus

- India Focus puts spotlight on the heritage, culture, customs, and history and geography of the Indian subcontinent.
- This provides students a deeper understanding of their homeland and creates a sense of solidarity.

Sustainable Development Goals

- The Sustainable Development Goals, adopted by the United Nations in 2015, are a collection of 17 interlinked global goals designed to achieve a better and more sustainable future for all by 2030. Here are the 17 goals:

Key Features

Page 71

Warm-up: A wide variety of theme-based activities with probing questions

Objectives: All learning goals for the chapter listed out

Page 15

Reading: A good balance of Indian and global selections from a wide range of literary genres that are useful in cross-curricular teaching

Comprehension: Covers factual, inferential, and extrapolative questions

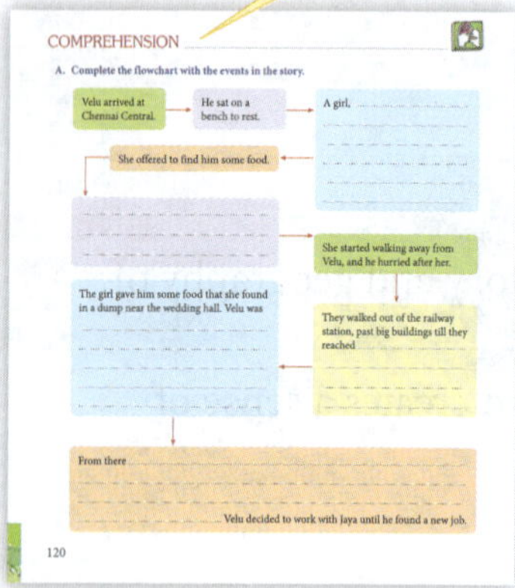

Page 120

Cross-curricular boxes: Topics related to other subjects highlighted

Glossary: Meanings for new words and literary devices given alongside the text

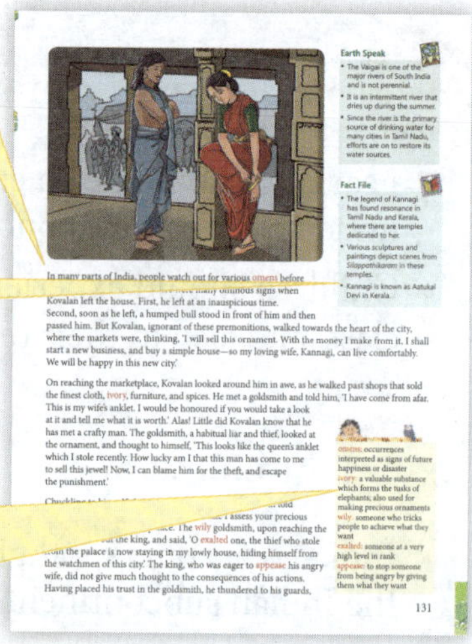

Page 131

Vocabulary: Covers language skills with focus on usage

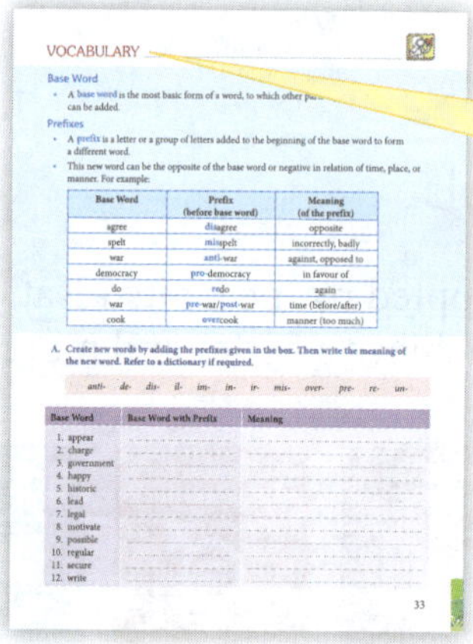

Page 33

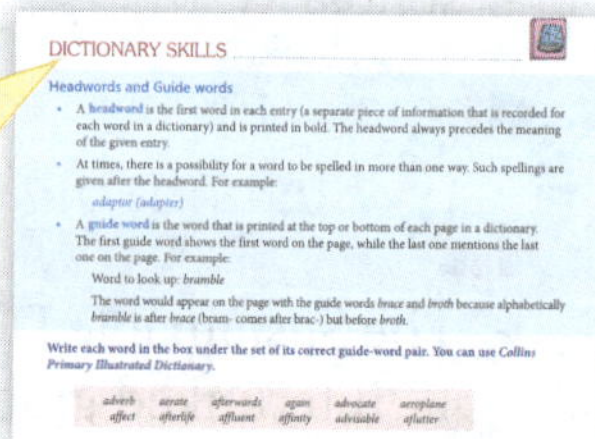

Page 22

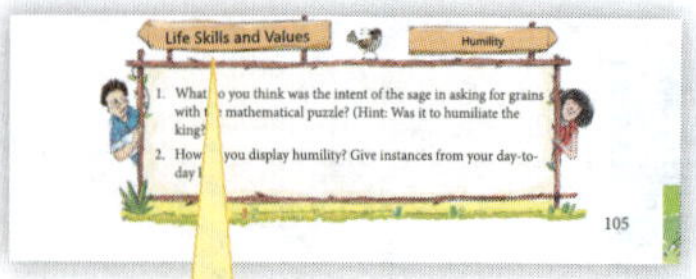

Page 105

Life Skills and Values: Value-based questions to develop good character through experiential learning

Summary: A short summary at the end of each text for a mental revision and an easier way of remembering the essence of the text

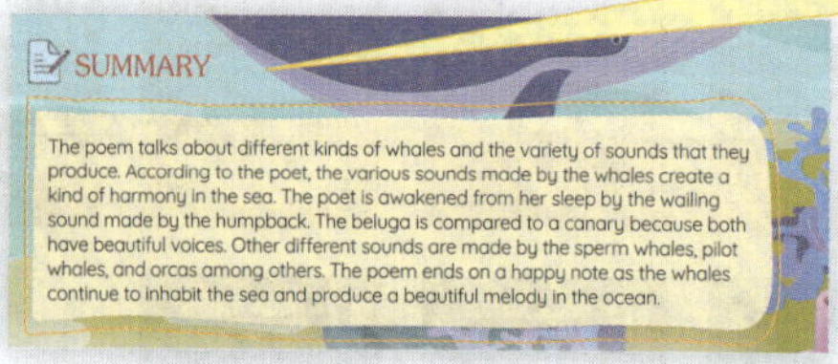

Page 66

Grammar: Grade-appropriate grammar explained with several visual models and extensive examples, followed by exercises

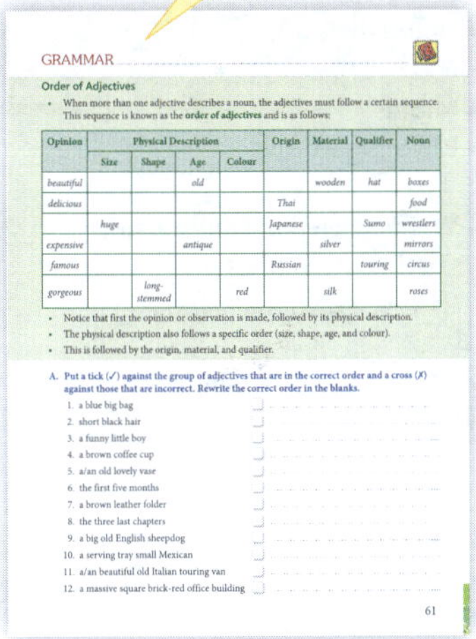

Page 61

Activity: A collaborative fun activity with each poem

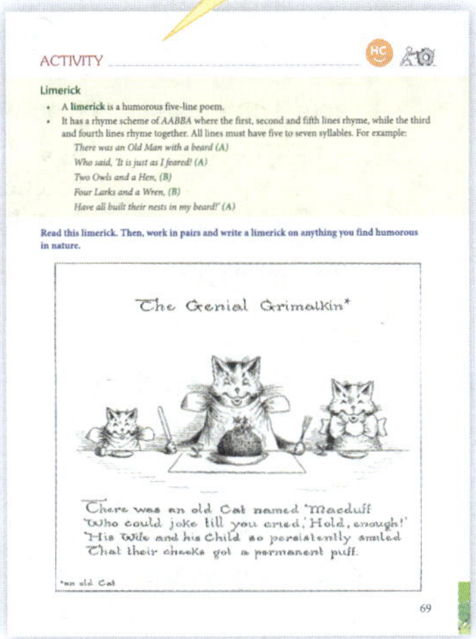

Page 69

Project: Three cross-curricular projects linked to topics taught in other subjects in this grade

Page 114

Listening and Speaking: A wide variety of communicative activities leading to collaboration and team building; also covers pronunciation

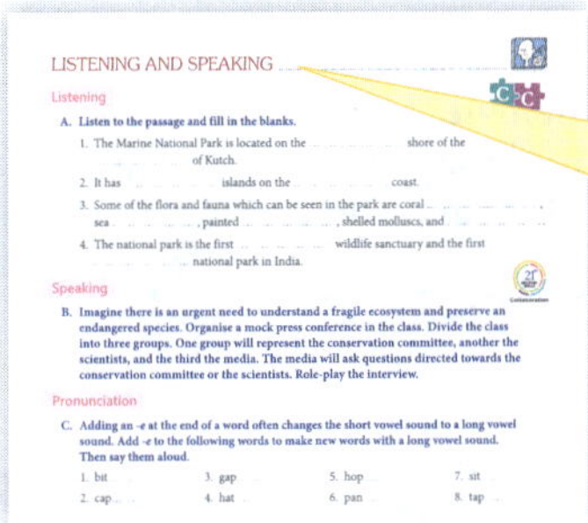

Page 54

Writing: A well-graded section with a variety of creative and scaffolded writing tasks

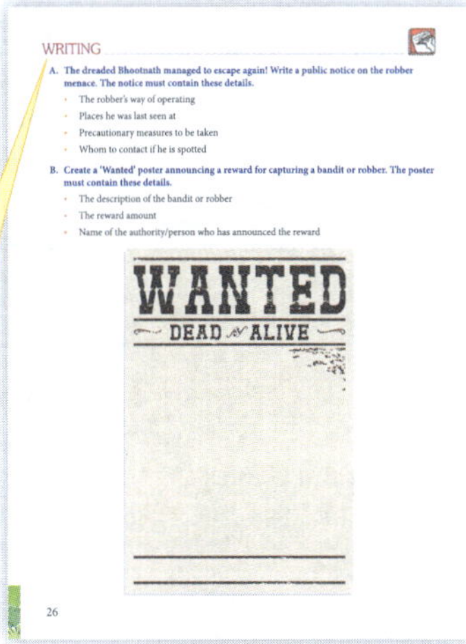

Page 26

Assessment Paper: A test paper provided at the end of the book to assess the end-of-year preparation and comprehension skills of the learners

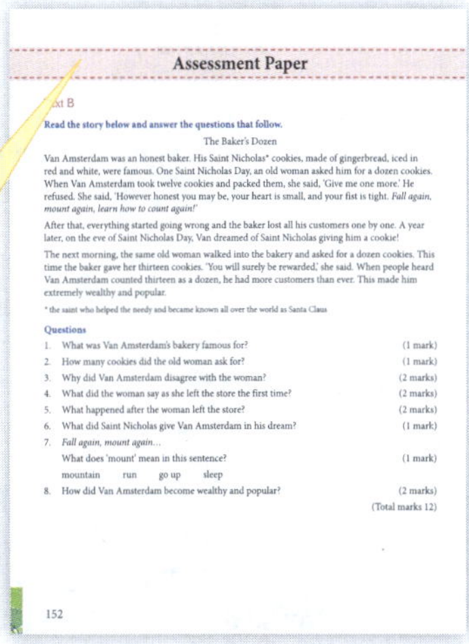

Page 152

*This series integrates the essence of **NIPUN Bharat** guidelines and the requirements of **Structured Assessments For Analyzing Learning (SAFAL)**.*

Detailed Contents

Grammar	Listening and Speaking	Writing	Activity
• Common, proper, and collective nouns **Punctuation:** Comma	• Listening to a story and sequencing the events • Enacting the story **Pronunciation:** Pronouncing silent letters	• Writing a public notice • Creating a 'Wanted' poster	
• Personal, possessive, and reflexive pronouns • Simple present, present continuous, and present perfect tenses	• Listening for information and gap-filling • Role-playing a dialogue **Pronunciation:** Syllable stress	• Writing an imaginary travelogue	
			• Conducting a tree survey
• Simple past tense • Adjectives • **Punctuation:** Apostrophe	• Listening for information and gap-filling • Role-playing a mock press conference **Pronunciation:** Short and long *e* vowel sounds	• Writing a newspaper article	
• Order of adjectives • Articles	• Listening for information and marking true or false • Sharing an experience in a conversation **Pronunciation:** Word stress	• Writing an email	
			• Writing a limerick
• Subject and predicate • Subject-verb agreement	• Listening to a passage and answering questions • Narrating a chain story	• Writing a diary entry	
• Transitive and intransitive verbs • Declarative, interrogative, imperative and exclamative sentences	• Listening to a passage and choosing the best answer • Speaking about overcoming a fear **Pronunciation:** Stress in compound nouns and compound words	• Writing a dialogue in the form of an interview	
			• Making a presentation on the origin of sign language • Reciting the poem like a rap
• Prepositions • Active and passive voice	• Listening to a passage and answering questions • Giving a motivational speech **Pronunciation:** Words ending with *-ed* and different sounds of *i*	• Writing a formal invitation	
			• Making a flow chart on the steps of building a tree house • Designing a new toy for Santa's toy factory
• Adverbs	• Sequencing and matching sentences • Class discussion **Pronunciation:** /s/ and /z/ sounds	• Writing an autobiography	
			• Conducting a survey
• Modals: *can, could, may, might, will, shall, should* and *must*	• Listening and matching the Indian epics with their incidents • Pair discussion	• Writing a short story	
• Future tense • Direct and indirect speech • Reporting verbs	• Listening to a passage and choosing the correct answer • Role-playing a conversation	• Writing a letter	

Contents

Unit 1: City and Country

WARM-UP

A. Read the statements. Identify whether the speaker is boasting or telling the truth.

1. There were many snakes in the snake pit in the zoo.
2. A big snake slithered into my lap and slept there.
3. There is a huge dragon behind the mountain near my village.
4. I hunted a tiger that was taller than an elephant when I went on a safari.
5. I was awestruck when a tiger came close to our jeep in the jungle.

B. Work in pairs and discuss.

1. Would you prefer to live in a city or the countryside? Why?
2. How is the city different from the countryside? Do you think the characteristics of the inhabitants differ in both?
3. Imagine you are moving to another city for a few years. If you were travelling to that city by train, which of the following items would you be able to carry along?

☐ almirah	☐ laptop	☐ suitcase
☐ bed	☐ parrot	☐ table
☐ books	☐ picnic hamper	☐ television
☐ board games	☐ potted plants	☐ tiger
☐ dog	☐ radio	☐ tortoise
☐ fruits	☐ snake	☐ toys
☐ gas cylinder	☐ squirrel	☐ water bottle
☐ headphones	☐ skateboard	☐ video games

Are all the above items allowed on a passenger train? If not, how would you move them to your new home?

C. Is it possible to adopt all these animals as pets? Why/Why not? Discuss in class.

D. Are trees important to us? Write down any six reasons that come to your mind.

Short story

1 Operation Blackbeard

–Aabid Surti

OBJECTIVES

In this chapter, we will:

- *read the story of a man who liked to boast.*
- *learn about the use of figurative language, synonyms, and antonyms.*
- *learn to find words in a dictionary using the headwords and guide words.*
- *learn about proper, common, and collective nouns; and to punctuate using a comma.*
- *listen to a story and sequence the order of events; enact the story with a different ending; and learn about silent letters.*
- *write a notice and make a poster.*

READING

HC

Have you met anyone who likes to boast all the time? Read what befell the boastful Nawab Rangile when he tried to capture the dreaded bandit Bhootnath.

He was indeed the great *Nawab* Jung Bahadur Rangile, even though he had never stepped on a battlefield, nor displayed any valour. His kingdom of Nagadpur was merged with India at the time of the Partition in 1947.

With time, not only did the princely lifestyle fade away, but the world around the *Nawab* turned topsy-turvy. Today, the great *Nawab* Rangile lives in a modest house with his wife, *Begum* Rangili, and does odd jobs like selling eggs and catching crooks.

One day, he was sitting under a tree narrating the story of his tiger hunt to a group of children.

Nawab: a Muslim nobleman, powerful landowner, or a person of high status
valour: great courage or bravery in the face of danger, especially in battle
topsy-turvy: in a confused or disorganised state
modest: (here) small
Begum: a Muslim woman of high rank
crooks: criminals or dishonest people

'With a sword in my hand, I chased the man-eater like a bullet. Sometimes, I was ahead of him, sometimes he was ahead of me!'

'Then what happened, *Nawab Sahib*?' a child asked excitedly.

'How dare the tiger defeat me? I ran so fast that after an hour, when I turned my head, the beast was nowhere to be seen!'

As the children broke out laughing, *Nawab* Rangile's friend Sher Singh appeared. Seeing his long face, *Nawab* Rangile asked, 'What's wrong, Shera?'

'Last night my house was burgled. Bhootnath, the bandit, has robbed my house clean and vanished.'

'Why did you not wake me up?'

'How could I? It was only when I woke up in the morning that I realised the loss.' Sher Singh cried. 'In fact, the bandit has plundered three more houses in the village!'

'What else can you expect from a village where a flock of cowards live?'

'True. But we do have a braveheart amongst us.'

'Indeed... that's me!'

'And that's why...' Sher Singh continued, 'Pukar Singh, the *mukhiya* has chosen you to go into the forest and catch Bhootnath.'

Nawab Rangile was shocked, for at the mention of the bandit's name, not only the village folks, but even the leaves trembled with fear. Somehow, he managed to put up a bold front and say, 'Who else could dare to enter that ghastly forest? I'll march into it tonight and bring him dragging to the village square before dawn.'

'That's the spirit... I did not... I mean... that is exactly what I expected from you. The *mukhiya* has announced a fabulous prize of ten thousand rupees to anyone who brings that crook to justice, dead or alive.'

Nawab Rangile closed his eyes and saw the cloud bursting with crisp, green, bank notes. Notes in the sky, notes in the air, notes everywhere. When he reached home, his heart sank. He thought of the bandit Bhootnath—big bulging eyes, frightening moustache, thick black beard and a wrestler's body. The truth was, alas, that no one had ever seen Bhootnath in person.

Looking Back

- When India attained independence from the British, it was divided into two countries—India and Pakistan. This division is referred to as the Partition. During the Partition, many people moved to the two newly-formed countries and settled there.
- Many princely states, similar to the fictional Nagadpur in this story, became a part of the newly-formed country, India. As a result, the ruler of those states became figureheads and had no role in the administration of the state.

Literary Device

- *put up a bold front*
  This is an example of an **idiom**. It means to appear to be brave (even if one is not).
- *his heart sank*
  This idiom means his courage failed and he felt less confident.

Sahib: an Urdu word for *Sir*
long face: a sad facial expression
burgled: robbed
plundered: robbed thoroughly by force
mukhiya: a Hindi word for *village headman*

Begum Rangili was worried to see her husband look so dismal and asked what was wrong.

'Bandit Bhootnath...' said *Nawab Sahib*.

Begum Rangili correctly guessed, 'He must have accepted the challenge to capture Bhootnath and now was cursing himself for his blunder.'

'Ah...' she said, 'So my valiant soldier is all set to launch Operation Blackbeard.'

Nawab Rangile was hurt. 'That bandit has done no harm to us, has he? Probably, he has realised this house is invincible. That is why he has never dared to touch us.'

'But will you go into the forest or...'

'Still plenty of time till sunset.'

After sunset, it was time to leave for the jungle, and poor *Nawab* Rangile was scared. He decided to hide under the bed, and told his wife his plan, 'If Shera comes to fetch me, tell him I have already left for the battlefield, fully armed.'

But Sher Singh had already arrived and was listening quietly from the door. '*Nawab Sahib*, the battlefield for bravehearts is not under the bed.' So saying, he led the *Nawab* out to meet the villagers who walked with them to the forest.

Despite his pounding heart, *Nawab* Rangile walked into the forest. He scampered up a tree to protect himself. The bandit Bhootnath had also chosen the same tree to get some sleep. Bhootnath woke up with a start, and asked, 'Who's there? Man or mouse?'

Feeling insulted, the *Nawab* replied, 'I am the original braveheart, *Nawab* Jung Bahadur Rangile of Nagadpur. I have sworn to catch Bhootnath and take him to the village to hang him. Who are you?'

'I am Lallu, the sweet-seller. I have also come in search of Bhootnath. Now, what is the use of spending the night here? It's better that I leave...'

The *Nawab* was terrified at the thought of the man leaving. He said, 'If I succeed in this venture, I will gift the prize money to you. To be honest, all the gold of my *Begum* is still safe in the house.'

Hearing the *Nawab*, a plan formed in the crafty bandit's mind. Bhootnath decided to steal the *Begum's* jewellery. He said, 'I don't think Bhootnath will dare come here tonight because the Braveheart is personally here. Let's go home and sleep in peace.'

Literary Device

Operation Blackbeard
This is an example of an **allusion**. Blackbeard was an infamous English pirate in the early eighteenth century in and around the Caribbean Islands. Here *Begum* Rangili is alluding to Bhootnath as Blackbeard, as both loot others.

dismal: sad and gloomy; without any hope
blunder: a silly or careless mistake
valiant: brave
invincible: too strong or powerful to be defeated
pounding: beating loudly
scampered: moved quickly with small light steps, especially through fear or excitement
sworn: pledged; promised
venture: a difficult activity involving a lot of risk
crafty: clever at achieving one's aims usually in a dishonest manner

Relieved, the *Nawab* invited Lallu home for dinner, took him home and introduced him to his *Begum*, 'This poor guy has not eaten anything for the last couple of days. Quick, make *halwa puri* as fast as you can.'

The *Begum* asked, 'You did not say anything about the bandit?'

'What is there to say?' There was a ringing tone of success in his voice. 'When he found out that I was looking for him, he simply vanished.'

But *Begum* Rangili was not that easy to fool. She had become alert the moment she had a glimpse of the guest. 'There is something dubious about the chap. The *Nawab* says he's a sweet-seller. But who has ever seen a sweet-seller with a hard, threatening face?'

Begum Rangili quickly realised who the guest was. But what could she do? She thought and thought. Then she spotted the *Nawab's* old sleeping pills. She mixed them in the *halwa* meant for the bandit, and carried two plates to the seated men.

'Lallu*ji*, the *halwa puri* dish, prepared by the master chef, *Begum* Rangili of Lucknow, is internationally known for its flavour and taste.' *Nawab* Bahadur had jumped up and served the man the unadulterated dish before she could wink at him. The *Begum* felt like banging her head on the wall. To make matters worse, the *Nawab* insisted on feeding his wife. Her protests fell on deaf ears, and she was forced to eat from the same dish as her husband's.

'You are a sweet-seller, have you ever cooked such a delicious dish?' the *Nawab* asked Bhootnath.

'Not even my father prepared anything like this.'

The *Nawab* stretched his legs on a *charpai*. He could not even finish his sentence and was soon fast asleep. In the kitchen, the *Begum* too was feeling dizzy. She was cursing herself for her ingenious idea. Soon, she too was sleeping like a log.

Bhootnath was quietly watching the scene. A miracle, he thought. Soon, he was at work. Quickly, he opened the safe, grabbed the jewellery box, and walked out through the front door like a gentleman.

halwa: an Indian sweet dish made with semolina, milk, and nuts
puri: an Indian deep-fried bread served with vegetables or *halwa*
dubious: suspicious; not to be considered completely safe or honest
unadulterated: completely pure without anything substandard added to it
fell on deaf ears: were ignored
charpai: a Hindi word for *woven cots* used in villages
ingenious: clever or inventive (but here, it is used to mean the opposite)
miracle: a very wonderful and surprising event that is unexpected

SUMMARY

The village of Nagadpur, where *Nawab* Rangile lived with his wife, was terrorised by the bandit, Bhootnath. *Nawab* Rangile, who always bragged about his own bravery, was assigned the task of capturing the bandit. While the *Nawab* hid in the forest to escape the dreaded bandit, coincidentally, they met each other. However, the bandit made him believe that he was just a poor sweet-seller. The *Nawab* took the bandit home, where his wife recognised him for who he was. She devised a clever plan to capture Bhootnath. Nonetheless, her efforts were thwarted by the gullible *Nawab*, who fed her the *halwa puri* that was mixed with sleeping pills. The poor *Nawab* was looted by the bandit.

About the Author

Aabid Surti (born 1935) is a national award-winning Indian author and playwright. He is also an accomplished painter and cartoonist. His cartoon strip about a simpleton called *Dhabbuji* is one of the most loved Hindi cartoons in India. He has written more than 80 books including short stories, novels, travelogues, plays and stories for children in Gujarati, Hindi, and English. He also writes film scripts, and articles for Hindi and Gujarati magazines and newspapers.

COMPREHENSION

A. Choose the best answer.

1. *Nawab* Rangile thought himself to be the ruler of
   a. Lucknow.
   b. Nagadpur.
   c. Hyderabad.
2. The *Nawab's* friend was
   a. Lallu.
   b. Sher Singh.
   c. Bhootnath.
3. The entire village feared
   a. Sher Singh.
   b. Bhootnath.
   c. *Nawab* Rangile.
4. *Nawab* Rangile decided to
   a. kill Bhootnath.
   b. go to the forest.
   c. hide under his bed.
5. Lallu was actually
   a. Rangile.
   b. Bhootnath.
   c. Pukar Singh.

B. Answer these questions briefly.

1. What did *Nawab* Rangile tell the children?
2. What did Sher Singh tell *Nawab* Rangile?
3. What challenge did *Nawab* Rangile accept, and why?
4. What happened in the jungle?
5. What crafty plan did Bhootnath think of? Did he succeed in his plan?
6. How did *Begum* Rangili guess Lallu's identity?
7. What was *Begum* Rangili's plan?
8. How did *Nawab* Rangile foil his wife's plans to catch the bandit?

C. Think and answer the questions.

1. Do you think *Nawab* Rangile was a brave man? Support your answer with examples.
2. *Nawab* Rangile prided himself on being a *Nawab*. Was this true? Was he a commoner in the village, or its crowned ruler?
3. Who do you think was the cleverer of the two—the *Nawab* or his *Begum*? Why do you think so?
4. The story ends with Bhootnath walking out of *Nawab* Rangile's house 'like a gentleman'. Do you think Bhootnath was a gentleman? Give reasons to justify your answer.

Life Skills and Values

Honesty and discernment

1. *Nawab* Rangile often tells stories about himself that are not true. Do you think it is wrong to boast or make up stories? Give reasons for your answer.
2. Imagine your friend has baked a cake for the first time but it did not turn out so well. What would you say to him/her? If you were in your friend's place, what would you like to hear and in what manner?

VOCABULARY

Figurative Language

The term **figurative language** covers a wide range of literary devices that writers use to make their writing more interesting and lively. The most commonly used figurative language consists of idioms, similes, metaphors, personifications, and hyperboles.

- An **idiom** is a commonly used expression whose meaning is different from what each word in it means. For example:

  His heart sank.

- A **simile** compares two different things with a common trait, using 'like' or 'as'. For example:

  Her cheeks were as red as roses.

- A **metaphor** is used to compare two things that have something in common, and to show a similarity. For example:

  The classroom is a zoo.

- **Imagery** describes something in detail to create a word picture for the reader. For example:

  Nawab Rangile closed his eyes and saw the cloud bursting with crisp, green, bank notes.

- **Personification** is a figure of speech in which a non-living thing or an object is given life-like qualities. For example:

  The wind howled through the windows.

- **Hyperbole** is an exaggeration used to create emphasis or effect. For example:

  We waited for centuries for the latest video game.

A. Match each sentence with its figure of speech.

Figure of Speech	Sentence
1. hyperbole	a. She was *sleeping like a log.*
2. idiom	b. It was *dark and dim in the forest.*
3. imagery	c. *Lightning danced* across the sky.
4. metaphor	d. It was so cold that *polar bears would wear jackets.*
5. personification	e. If Shera comes to fetch me, tell him I have already *left for the battlefield, fully armed.*
6. simile	f. Lara is going to be *in hot water* when her mother finds out she has broken the antique vase.

Synonyms and Antonyms

B. Write the synonyms of these words.

1. blunder ....
2. burgle ....
3. modest ....
4. plunder ....
5. scampered ....
6. valour ....

C. Match the words with their antonyms.

Word	Antonym
1. delicious	a. appear
2. ingenious	b. courageous
3. quickly	c. failure
4. scared	d. foolish
5. success	e. slowly
6. vanish	f. tasteless

DICTIONARY SKILLS

Headwords and Guide words

- A **headword** is the first word in each entry (a separate piece of information that is recorded for each word in a dictionary) and is printed in bold. The headword always precedes the meaning of the given entry.
- At times, there is a possibility for a word to be spelled in more than one way. Such spellings are given after the headword. For example:

  adaptor (adapter)
- A **guide word** is the word that is printed at the top or bottom of each page in a dictionary. The first guide word shows the first word on the page, while the last one mentions the last one on the page. For example:

  Word to look up: *bramble*

  The word would appear on the page with the guide words *brace* and *broth* because alphabetically *bramble* is after *brace* (bram- comes after brac-) but before *broth*.

Write each word in the box under the set of its correct guide-word pair. You can use *Collins Primary Illustrated Dictionary*.

adverb *aerate* *afterwards* *again* *advocate* *aeroplane*
affect *afterlife* *affluent* *affinity* *advisable* *aflutter*

aerodrome—afford	afforestation—against	adventurer—aerobic

GRAMMAR

Common and Proper Nouns

- **Common nouns** are the names given to general things, animals, places, or people. For example:

  The children sat under a tree in a village.

- **Proper nouns** are specific names given to individual people, animals, places, or things. For example:

  Nawab Rangile lived in Nagadpur.

A. Underline the common nouns and circle the proper nouns in the following sentences.

1. Sher Singh was a clever man.
2. The children liked to play near the forest.
3. The guest ate the *halwa puri* that was served at the house.
4. *Nawab* Rangile lived in a small village with his wife, *Begum* Rangili.
5. Bhootnath was a dreaded bandit who plundered houses in Nagadpur.
6. India was divided into many princely states before the British occupied it.

Collective Nouns

- **Collective nouns** are words that refer to a collection of people or things, and they are usually treated as a whole. For example:

  A flock of geese flew over the lake.

B. Fill in the blanks using the correct collective nouns.

army congress sleuth pack parliament pride

1. an .... of ants
2. a .... of baboons
3. a .... of bears
4. a .... of owls
5. a .... of tigers
6. a .... of wolves

C. Complete the sentences using the collective nouns from the box.

crew flock heap herd pack swarm

1. We saw a .... of sheep grazing on the hillside.
2. The .... of the aircraft was polite and courteous.

3. A .... of wolves attacked a .... of deer.
4. A .... of dirty clothes was piled up in a corner of the room.
5. There was a .... of bees hovering over the flowers in the garden.

Punctuation

Comma

- A **comma** is used to split a sentence into meaningful segments. For example:
  The great Nawab Rangile, who was the erstwhile ruler of Nagadpur, sold eggs for a living.
- It is also used to denote clauses. For example:
  He decided to hide under the bed, and told his wife his plan.
- Commas are also used in lists between nouns or adjectives.
  I have to buy butter, eggs, lemons, and sugar.

D. Insert commas wherever necessary.

1. The villages where the farmers lived had few modern facilities.
2. The man drove a car which was gifted to him by his grandfather.
3. He went to the market and bought eggs milk meat fruits and vegetables.
4. These men the original bravehearts have given up their medals as a form of protest.
5. One day he was sitting under a tree narrating the story of his tiger hunt to a group of children.
6. Though Rima was suffering from fever she didn't miss any exam.
7. In addition to English I also want to learn Mandarin French Spanish and German.
8. Whenever I feel bored I pick up a pen and start writing about the most interesting incidents of my life.

E. Read the passage, and punctuate it appropriately by inserting commas, full stops, and capital letters wherever necessary.

Bhavya my best friend is coming over to spend the summer vacation with me we will have a lot of fun together. we plan to visit nainital ranikhet almora and kausani. We will visit the zoo see sites go shopping and go for a boat ride in nainital bhavya wants to buy trinkets and local handicrafts at the mall road woodcraft market as gifts for her cousins friends and neighbours. Like nainital ranikhet almora and kausani are also hill stations and remain comparatively cool even during the summer months It will be refreshing to visit these cool peaceful and beautiful places in the lap of the himalayas.

LISTENING AND SPEAKING

Listening

A. Listen to a story about a king who had unusually big ears. Order the events mentioned in the correct sequence.

- ☐ A Raja had big ears.
- ☐ He wanted a haircut.
- ☐ A woodcutter cut the tree.
- ☐ Everybody knew the Raja's secret.
- ☐ He finally told his secret to a tree in the forest.
- ☐ A flute was made from the wood, cut from the tree.
- ☐ When played, the flute sang, 'The Raja has big ears.'
- ☐ The Raja told the barber that he must not tell anyone.
- ☐ He almost told his wife that the Raja had big ears, but changed it to earrings.
- ☐ The barber almost told his customer about the Raja, but he changed his words and said that the Raja had big rings.

Speaking

B. Do you think that the story, *Operation Blackbeard*, could have ended differently? Work in groups and enact the story with a different ending.

Pronunciation

Silent letter

A **silent letter** in a word is one that is written but not pronounced. For example:

the *b* in *debt*	the *k* in *knees*	the *l* in *half*	the *n* in *column*
the *r* in *first*	the *s* in *island*	the *t* in *listen*	the *w* in *wrecked*

C. Read out the following words aloud, and circle the silent letter in each one.

1. doubt
2. thumb
3. comb
4. palm
5. knot
6. know
7. knock
8. calf
9. yolk
10. autumn
11. hymn
12. debris
13. castle
14. soften
15. write
16. whole

WRITING

A. The dreaded Bhootnath managed to escape again! Write a public notice on the robber menace. The notice must contain these details.

- The robber's way of operating
- Places he was last seen at
- Precautionary measures to be taken
- Whom to contact if he is spotted

B. Create a 'Wanted' poster announcing a reward for capturing a bandit or robber. The poster must contain these details.

- The description of the bandit or robber
- The reward amount
- Name of the authority/person who has announced the reward

2 Travelling with Grandfather's Zoo

–Ruskin Bond

OBJECTIVES

In this chapter, we will:

- *read the story about funny pet adventures.*
- *learn about base words, prefixes, and suffixes.*
- *learn about pronouns, the simple present, present continuous, and present perfect tenses.*
- *listen to a passage for details, enact a role-play, and practise pronouncing the words with weak a sound.*
- *write an imaginary story.*

READING

HC

Do you have pets or would you like to have pets? Read about the adventures that take place when a family decides to travel with their exotic and uncommon pets.

'All aboard!' shrieked Popeye, Grandmother's pet parrot, as the family climbed aboard the *Lucknow Express*.

We were moving for some months from Dehra to Lucknow, and as Grandmother had insisted on taking her parrot along, Grandfather and I insisted on bringing our pets too—a teenaged tiger (Grandfather's) and a small squirrel (mine). But we thought it prudent to leave the python behind.

In those days, trains in India were not so crowded and it was possible to travel with a variety of creatures. Grandfather had decided to do things in style by travelling first-class; so, we had a four-berth compartment of our own, and Timothy, the tiger, had an entire berth to himself.

Later, everyone agreed that Timothy behaved perfectly throughout the journey. Even the guard admitted that he could not have asked for a better passenger: no stealing from vendors, no shouting at coolies, no breaking of railway property, no spitting on the platform.

All aboard: a warning call made to passengers of a bus, ship, or train when ready for departure
prudent: sensible and careful in avoiding risks; cautious

All the same, the journey was not without incident and before we reached Lucknow, there was excitement enough for everyone.

To begin with, Popeye objected to vendors and other people poking their hands in through the windows. Before the train had moved out of the Dehra station, he had nipped two fingers and tweaked a ticket inspector's ear.

No sooner had the train started moving than Chips, my squirrel, emerged from my pocket to examine his surroundings. Before I could stop him, he was out of the compartment door, scurrying along the corridor.

Chips discovered that the train was a squirrel's paradise, almost all the passengers having bought large quantities of roasted peanuts before the train pulled out. He had no difficulty in making friends with both children and grown-ups, and it was an hour before he returned to our compartment, his tummy almost bursting.

'I think I'll go to sleep,' said Grandmother, covering herself with a blanket and stretching out on the berth opposite Timothy's. 'It's been a tiring day.'

'Aren't you going to eat anything?' asked Grandfather.

'I'm not hungry—I had some soup before we left. You two help yourselves from the tiffin basket.'

Grandmother dozed off, and even Popeye started nodding, lulled to sleep by the clackety-clack of the wheels and the steady puffing of the steam engine.

'Well, I'm hungry,' I said. 'What did Granny make for us?'

'Sandwiches, boiled eggs, a roast chicken, gooseberry pie. It's all in the tiffin basket under your berth.'

I tugged at the large basket and dragged it into the centre of the compartment. The straps were loosely tied. No sooner had I undone them than the lid flew open, and I let out a gasp of surprise. In the basket was Grandfather's pet python, curled up contentedly on the remains of our dinner.

Grandmother had insisted that we leave the python behind, and Grandfather had let it loose in the garden. Somehow, it had managed to snuggle itself into the tiffin basket.

'Well, what are you staring at?' asked Grandfather from his corner.

'It's the python,' I said. 'And it has finished all our dinner.'

Looking Back

- The Indian Railways was founded on 16 April 1853, when the first passenger train ran between Bombay and Thane. The fourteen carriages were pulled by three steam engines, and carried 400 passengers. It took 45 minutes to cover a distance of 34 km.
- Today, the Indian Railways is the largest railway network in Asia.

nipped: bit sharply
tweaked: pulled or twisted sharply with a sudden movement
emerged: came out
scurrying: moving hurriedly with quick short steps
tiffin basket: a picnic basket with a lid, used for carrying light meal or snacks on long journeys
contentedly: happily; expressing satisfaction
remains: (here) leftovers; what is left after part has been used
snuggle: settle into a warm and comfortable position

Grandfather joined me, and together we looked down at what remained of the food. Pythons don't chew, they swallow: outlined along the length of the large snake's sleek body were the distinctive shapes of a chicken, a pie, and six boiled eggs. We couldn't make out the sandwiches, but presumably these had been eaten too because there was no sign of them in the basket. Only a few apples remained. Evidently, the python did not care for apples.

Grandfather snapped the basket shut and pushed it back beneath the berth.

'We mustn't let Grandmother see him,' he said.

'She might think we brought him along on purpose.'

'Well, I'm hungry,' I complained.

Just then, Chips returned from one of his forays and presented me with a peanut.

'Thanks,' I said. 'If you keep bringing me peanuts all night, I might last until morning.'

But it was not long before I felt sleepy.

Grandfather had begun to nod and the only one who was wide awake was the squirrel, still intent on investigating distant compartments.

A little after midnight there was a great clamour at the end of the corridor. Grandfather and I woke up. Timothy growled in his sleep, and Popeye made complaining noises. Suddenly there were cries of '*Saanp*! *Saanp*!'

Grandfather was on his feet in a moment. He looked under the berth. The tiffin basket was empty. 'The python's out!' he said, and dashed out of our compartment in his pyjamas. I was close behind.

About a dozen passengers were bunched together outside the washroom door.

'Anything wrong?' asked Grandfather casually.

'We can't get into the toilet,' said someone.

'There's a huge snake inside.'

'Let me take a look,' said Grandfather. 'I know all about snakes.'

The passengers made way for him, and he entered the washroom to find the python curled up in the washbasin. After its heavy meal it had become thirsty and finding the lid of the tiffin basket easy to pry up, had set out in search of water.

Grandfather gathered up the sleepy, overfed python and stepped out of the washroom. The passengers hastily made way for them.

Science Scan

- Pythons are very large snakes that are not poisonous. They are constrictors, which means that they kill their prey by wrapping themselves around it and squeezing it till it stops breathing.
- Pythons swallow their prey in one single piece and may take several weeks to digest it. Thus, they usually feed only when required.
- Pythons can survive in tropical rainforests, savannahs, and deserts.

distinctive: special feature or quality that makes something easy to recognise
presumably: very likely
forays: short visits with a purpose
intent: intention or purpose; determined to do something
clamour: a loud noise made by a large group of people shouting or talking together
saanp: a Hindi word for *snake*
pry up: use force to move apart or open something
hastily: hurriedly

'Nothing to worry about,' said Grandfather cheerfully. 'It's just a harmless young python. He's had his dinner already, so no one is in any danger!'

And he marched back to our compartment with the python in his arms. As soon as I was inside, he bolted the door. Grandmother was sitting up on her berth.

'I knew you'd do something foolish behind my back,' she scolded. 'You told me you'd got rid of that creature, and all the time you've been hiding it from me.'

Grandfather tried to explain that we had nothing to do with it, that the python had smuggled itself into the tiffin basket, but Grandmother was unconvinced. 'What will Mabel do when she sees it?' she cried despairingly.

My Aunt Mabel was a schoolteacher in Lucknow. She was going to share our new house, and she was terrified of all reptiles, particularly snakes.

'We won't let her see it,' said Grandfather.

'Back it goes into the tiffin basket.'

Early next morning, the train steamed into Lucknow. Aunt Mabel was on the platform to receive us. Grandfather let all the other passengers get off before he emerged from the compartment with Timothy on a chain. I had Chips in my pocket, suitcase in both hands. Popeye stayed perched on Grandmother's shoulder, eyeing the busy platform with considerable distrust.

Aunt Mabel, a lover of good food, immediately spotted the tiffin basket, picked it up and said, 'It's not very heavy. I'll carry it out to the taxi. I hope you've kept something for me.'

'A whole chicken,' I said.

'We hardly ate anything,' said Grandfather.

'It's all yours, Aunty!' I added.

smuggled: (here) secretly moved in
unconvinced: not certain if something is true
despairingly: hopelessly

'Oh, good!' exclaimed Aunt Mabel. 'It's been ages since I tasted something cooked by your grandmother.' And after that there was no getting the basket away from her.

Glancing at it, I thought I saw the lid bulging, but Grandfather had tied it down quite firmly this time and there was little likelihood of its suddenly bursting open.

An enormous 1950 Chevrolet taxi was waiting outside the station, and the family tumbled into it. Timothy got onto the back seat, leaving enough room for Grandfather and me. Aunt Mabel sat in front with Grandmother, the tiffin basket on her lap.

'Tell the taxi driver where to take us, dear,' said Grandmother. He's looking rather nervous.' Aunt Mabel gave instructions to the driver, and the taxi shot off in a cloud of dust.

'Well, here we go!' said Grandfather. 'I'm looking forward to settling into the new house.' Popeye, perched proudly on Grandmother's shoulder, kept one suspicious eye on the quivering tiffin basket. 'All aboard!' he squawked. 'All aboard!'

When we got to our new house, we found a light breakfast waiting for us on the dining table.

'It isn't much,' said Aunt Mabel. 'But we'll supplement it with the contents of your hamper.' And placing the basket on the table, she removed the lid. The python was half-asleep, with an apple in its mouth. As soon as she saw it, Aunt Mabel fainted away.

Grandfather promptly picked up the python, took it into the garden, and placed it over a branch of a guava tree.

When Aunt Mabel recovered, she insisted that there was a huge snake in the tiffin basket. We showed her the empty basket.

'You're seeing things,' said Grandfather.

'It must be the heat,' I said.

Grandmother said nothing. But Popeye broke into shrieks of maniacal laughter, and soon everyone, including a slightly hysterical Aunt Mabel, was doubled up with laughter.

Chevrolet: an American car brand
tumbled: (here) climbed quickly and clumsily
quivering: trembling or shaking slightly
hamper: a large basket with a lid, used for carrying food in
maniacal: extremely loud and wild
hysterical: in a state of uncontrolled excitement, anger, or panic

SUMMARY

This story is about a train trip that the author and his grandparents took from Dehra to Lucknow. Their travelling companions were their pets; a tiger, a talking parrot, and a squirrel. They had decided to leave their pet python behind because Aunt Mabel, with whom they would be staying in Lucknow, was afraid of reptiles. However, the python had somehow slid into their picnic basket, and was discovered only when the author and his grandfather opened the hamper to have their dinner. Later, there was a commotion when the python escaped and went into the train's washroom as it was thirsty. Grandfather took the python back to the basket and kept it secure. Aunt Mabel, who received them at the railway station, kept the hamper with her since she was blissfully unaware of its contents. When she finally opened the hamper and saw the python, she fainted. Grandfather took the python and placed it over a tree branch in the garden and joked that Mabel was seeing things, in order to lighten the situation.

About the Author

Ruskin Bond (born 1934) is an Indian author of British origin. His novels, poems, short stories, and essays display his love for nature, particularly the mountains. He wrote his first novel, *The Room on the Roof*, at the age of 17 and won the John Llewellyn Rhys prize for it. He has also won the Sahitya Academy Award, the Padma Shri and the Padma Bhushan. His literary works include *The Angry River, Rain in the Mountains*, and *Scenes from a Writer's Life*. Award-winning films have been made based on his original stories, *A Flight of Pigeons*, and *The Blue Umbrella*.

COMPREHENSION

A. Match the names with the characters.

Name	Character
1. Chips	a. tiger
2. Timothy	b. parrot
3. Popeye	c. squirrel

B. Answer these questions briefly.

1. Where was the narrator going?
2. Who were the narrator's travelling companions? What was strange about them?
3. How was Timothy better behaved than most passengers?
4. What happened to the family's dinner?
5. Who was their unwelcomed companion? What did Grandfather do to it?
6. Why was there a commotion in the train?
7. Why did Grandmother scold Grandfather?
8. What happened when Aunt Mabel opened the lid of the basket?

C. Think and answer the questions.

1. Do you think the animals enjoyed their train journey? Give reasons for your answer.
2. Pick out a few humorous incidents from the story.
3. The author attributes human qualities to the animals in the story. Pick out a few such examples. What does this show about the author's feelings for animals?
4. Write a character sketch of Aunt Mabel.

Life Skills and Values

Handling crisis

1. What can we learn from the way Grandfather handled crisis situations in the story? What would you have done had you discovered a python in the train's washroom?
2. Do you think travelling with pets require special care? What, according to you, can be done to ensure safety for pets while travelling?

VOCABULARY

Base Word

- A **base word** is the most basic form of a word, to which other parts—prefixes or suffixes—can be added.

Prefixes

- A **prefix** is a letter or a group of letters added to the beginning of the base word to form a different word.
- This new word can be the opposite of the base word or negative in relation of time, place, or manner. For example:

Base Word	Prefix (before base word)	Meaning (of the prefix)
agree	**dis**agree	opposite
spelt	**mis**spelt	incorrectly, badly
war	**anti**-war	against, opposed to
democracy	**pro**-democracy	in favour of
do	**re**do	again
war	**pre**-war/**post**-war	time (before/after)
cook	**over**cook	manner (too much)

A. Create new words by adding the prefixes given in the box. Then write the meaning of the new word. Refer to a dictionary if required.

anti- *de-* *dis-* *il-* *im-* *in-* *ir-* *mis-* *over-* *pre-* *re-* *un-*

Base Word	Base Word with Prefix	Meaning
1. appear	....	....
2. charge	....	....
3. government	....	....
4. happy	....	....
5. historic	....	....
6. lead	....	....
7. legal	....	....
8. motivate	....	....
9. possible	....	....
10. regular	....	....
11. secure	....	....
12. write	....	....

Suffixes

- A **suffix** is a letter or a group of letters added to the end of the base word to form a different word.
- This new word is usually of a different grammatical type. For example:

Base Word	Suffix (after base word)	Change in Word Type
forget	forget**ful**	changes verb to adjective
industrial	industrial**ise**	changes adjective to verb
beauty	beauti**fy**	changes noun to verb
govern	govern**ment**	changes verb to noun
calm	calm**ly**	changes verb to adverb

- Often the spelling of the base word needs to be changed when adding a suffix. Here are some rules:
  - *-y* changes to *i*, for example:
    beauty + ful → beautiful
    heavy + ness → heaviness
  - *-le* changes to *il*, for example:
    able + ity → ability
  - *-e* changes to *ion*, for example:
    complicate + ion → complication
  - *-t* changes to *ss*, for example:
    permit + ion → permission

B. Create new words by adding the suffixes given in the box. Also write the change in the word type from the original base word. Refer to a dictionary if required.

-dom -ful -hood -ify -ity -ise -less -ly -ness -sion -tion -y

Base Word	Base Word with Suffix	Change in Word Type
1. class	....	....
2. memory	....	....
3. child	....	....
4. easy	....	....
5. equal	....	....
6. express	....	....
7. forget	....	....
8. happy	....	....
9. home	....	....
10. king	....	....
11. populate	....	....
12. wind	....	....

GRAMMAR

Pronouns

- A **pronoun** is a word used in place of a noun that has already been mentioned. It is used to avoid repetition.

Personal pronouns

- **Personal pronouns** such as *I*, *me*, *you*, *him*, *her*, *we*, *us*, *they*, and *them* show both person and number.
- The personal pronouns *he*, *she*, *him*, and *her* also show gender.
- We use *it* to refer to things, countries, vehicles, and machines.

Possessive pronouns

- **Possessive pronouns** such as *my*, *mine*, *your*, *yours*, *his*, *hers*, *our*, *ours*, *it*, *their*, and *theirs* are used to show possession and belonging.
- We should avoid using *its* and *one's* as possessive pronouns except when using them with *own*. For example:

  The house had a life of its own.
- Never use *'s* after possessive pronouns, especially with *its*. *It's* is a contraction of *it is*.

Reflexive pronouns

- **Reflexive pronouns** always end in *-self* or *-selves*, such as *myself*, *yourself*, *himself*, *herself*, *itself*, *oneself*, *ourselves*, *yourselves*, and *themselves*.
- They refer back to the subject forms of the personal pronouns.

A. Fill in the blanks with the correct pronouns.

1. Where's the key? I can't find ....
2. I cut .... on the broken glass.
3. Your dress is very similar to ....
4. Naina loves to run. .... runs daily.
5. My uncle is coming to visit .... this winter.
6. Grandfather was on .... feet in a moment.
7. I'm going to get .... hair cut this weekend.
8. Rohan, could you please pass me .... spectacles?
9. Would you like to join .... for a walk on the beach?
10. She makes .... a cup of coffee before sitting down to watch her favourite show.

Simple Present Tense

The **simple present tense** is used:

- to talk about general truths and facts. For example:

  Mrs Basu doesn't teach me, but she teaches my brother.

  Do you live in Hossur? My uncle lives there too.
- to talk about regular habits. For example:

  I swim every evening.
- to give instructions or directions. For example:

  Take the train to the city centre, and then take the bus to the museum.
- to describe a series of actions as they happen, either in a novel or in sports commentaries. For example:

  Eric fouls Messi. Messi takes the free kick. David blocks.
- to talk about immediate reactions or feelings. For example:

  I love this colour. I think you look very lovely.
- to talk about events that are part of a timetable or future plan. For example:

  The class starts at 10:00 a.m. *tomorrow instead of 9:30 a.m.*

There are some simple spelling rules when using the simple present tense. They are:

- add *-s* to the base form of the verb when using the third person singular (*he, she, it* forms). For example:

Third Person Singular	Base Verb + *s*
he/she/it	*eats* *reads* *travels*

- For other verbs, the spelling rules are:

Base Verb	*he/she/it*
Add *-es* at the end of the base verb, if it ends in *-ch*, *-ss*, *-sh*, *-x*, or *-zz*.	*watches* *misses* *washes* *mixes* *buzzes*
When the base verb ends in a consonant + *-y*, change *-y* to *-i* and add *-es*.	*hurry* → *hurries* *study* → *studies*
When the base verb ends in a vowel + *-y*, just add *-s*.	*enjoy* → *enjoys*

- For irregular verbs, the spelling rules are:

Irregular Verb	*he/she/it*
be	*is*
have	*has*
go	*goes*
do	*does*

B. Fill in the blanks with the correct form of the verb in brackets.

1. Sumer .... (*swim*) regularly.
2. A lone bee .... (*buzz*) over the rose.
3. She .... (*go*) to the library every weekend.
4. I plan to .... (*visit*) all the major beaches in Goa.
5. Raspberries .... (*be*) slightly sour even when they ripen.
6. The dirty road .... (*branch*) off into the forest from the lake.
7. Our dog .... (*splash*) around in the pool during the summer.
8. The mother .... (*kiss*) the baby every night before putting her to bed.
9. Humans .... (*destroy*) the forests which are the habitats of many animals.
10. She .... (*box*) daily and .... (*practise*) hard to win the competition.

Present Continuous Tense

- The present continuous tense is used to:
  - talk about an event which is in progress at the time of speaking. For example:
    Father is cooking a special dinner tonight.
  - talk about temporary states which are happening during the time of speaking. For example:
    My grandmother is living with my aunt at the moment.
  - describe regular or repeated actions. For example:
    She's studying a lot these days.
  - talk about a gradual change. For example:
    They're building a new basketball court.
  - refer to future plans that have already been finalised. For example:
    We are moving to Hyderabad in March.
- Note that all the above examples use *am/are/is* + the *-ing* form of the verb.
- There are some simple spelling rules when using the present continuous tense.
  - In most cases, *-ing* is added to the base form of the verb. For example:
    be → being *do → doing* *go → going*

- If the base verb ends in *-e*, drop the *-e* before adding *-ing*. For example:

  come → coming *move → moving*

- If the base verb ends in a vowel followed by a single consonant, the consonant is doubled before adding *-ing*. For example:

  rub → rubbing *travel → travelling*

  However, this rule does not apply for the verbs *cover* and *remember*. For example:

  cover → covering *remember → remembering*

Present Perfect Tense

- The **present perfect tense** is used to talk about events in the past that are connected to the present. For example:

  I have visited my grandparents.

- It uses the *have/has* + the *-ed* form of the verb. For example:

  We have worked hard for the exams.

C. Identify if the underlined verbs are in the simple present, present continuous, or present perfect form.

1. Is the sun hot? ....
2. It has rained all day. ....
3. It rains in June and September. ....
4. They have travelled to many countries. ....
5. I am reading this book since yesterday. ....
6. The man is trying to establish a business. ....
7. She has practised regularly for the match. ....
8. The girls have dressed their dolls up beautifully. ....
9. We are baking a cake for our granny's sixtieth birthday. ....
10. He is cleaning the house for tonight's party. ....

LISTENING AND SPEAKING

Listening

A. Listen to this passage about another adventure that the narrator's family had. Fill in the blanks with appropriate words.

This is the story of Henry, our pet .... Although Henry did not cause any trouble in our house, he did create somewhat of a riot in the .... down the road. It started out quite innocently.

When the .... in our orchard were ripe, Grandmother sent a basketful to her friend, Mrs Ghosh, who was the .... of the nursery school. While the basket was waiting in our garden, Henry slipped in among the papayas. The ...., unaware of this, took the basket to the school and left it in Mrs Ghosh's office.

When Mrs Ghosh came back after her rounds, she saw Henry and started to .... A .... who came to her aid, also started screaming. This scared Henry, who ran into a .... The children ran in all ...., some to get away from him, and others, to catch him. Henry finally .... and came back to our ....

Speaking

B. Work in pairs and do a role-play. Imagine you are a passenger travelling in the first-class coach with the narrator and his family. Perform a dialogue between you and the narrator regarding his pets.

Pronunciation

C. Read the following words aloud. Pay attention to the first sound in each word.

1. about	3. allot	5. annoy	7. around
2. ago	4. amount	6. alone	8. astounding

In these words, the first syllable, denoted by the first *a*, is a weak syllable and is not stressed.

WRITING

21st Century Skills — Creative Thinking

Write a travelogue about an imaginary journey you took with your pets. Do include these points.

- **Introduction**
  - The place you travelled to
  - With whom you travelled
  - Your mode of transport
  - Your fellow passengers
- **Context**
  - Why you travelled with pets
  - What you packed to ensure safety
  - How your pets behaved on the trip
- **Build up**
  - A strange occurrence or a problematic situation
  - How it was solved
- **Conclusion**
  - The end of your journey
  - The mood of the travellers

3 Cypress Street

–Todd-Michael St. Pierre

OBJECTIVES

In this chapter, we will:

- *read the poem on deforestation.*
- *learn idiomatic sentences and identify rhyming pairs.*
- *conduct a tree survey, and prepare and present the report.*

READING

The cypress is an evergreen coniferous tree that grows in the northern temperate regions. If a street were named Cypress Tree, how would you imagine it looked like?

I took a stroll down Cypress Street
The hot sidewalk beneath my feet.

The one thing that stood out the most
Where trees once stood there were lampposts.

I'd never seen so much concrete
No Cypress left on Cypress Street.

According to my Great Aunt Gem
There used to be a lot of them.

stroll: walk in a slow, relaxed manner
sidewalk: American English for *pavement*
concrete: a substance used for constructing building and pavements

They cut them down. They took their wood
A treeless street is plum no good!

Just like a treeless neighbourhood

So tell the Mayor next time they meet...
To change the name to Lamppost Street!

Fact File

- Traditionally, the cypress is considered the symbol of mourning.
- They can often be found growing in cemeteries or growing in neatly arranged rows in mausoleums.
- The path that leads to the Taj Mahal has cypress growing on both its sides.

SUMMARY

This is an interesting poem that uses the innocence of a child to bring out the evils of deforestation for the sake of development. *Cypress Street*, so named for its beautiful trees, is at present, full of lampposts, and does not have a single cypress tree. Though the poet's aunt remembered trees on the street, this must have been long ago. The poet goes on to say that the street should be renamed *Lamppost Street* as one could only see lampposts instead of cypress trees. The poem makes us aware of how modernisation has affected nature.

About the Poet

Todd-Michael St. Pierre is an American author and storyteller. *Cypress Street* is from his collection *A Treehouse on the Moon*. His other works include *The Louisiana State Bird Beauty Pageant, Chicory and Roux,* and *A Wooly Mammoth on Amelia Street.*

COMPREHENSION

A. Read the lines from the poem and answer the questions.

1. *I'd never seen so much concrete*
   a. What is the poet talking about?
   b. Why was there so much concrete?
2. *There used to be a lot of them.*
   a. What is referred to as *a lot of them*?
   b. What happened to them?

B. Answer these questions briefly.

1. What was the poet doing?
2. What had taken the place of the trees?
3. What had happened to the trees?
4. What does the poet feel about a treeless street?
5. What does the poet want to convey to the mayor?

C. Think and answer the questions.

1. What message is the poet trying to convey through this poem?
2. Do you think the poet is disturbed by the turn of events? Quote any two lines from the poem to show it.

Life Skills and Values — Conservation and regeneration

1. We must continuously work towards protecting our environment. List five things that you can do daily towards environmental conservation.
2. Talk about the negative effects of deforestation. What all could you do if the trees in your locality are being cut down?

VOCABULARY

Idiom

- An **idiom** is a phrase that has a figurative meaning which is different from the meaning of the individual words in it.

A. Read these idiomatic sentences.

1. He sees himself going right to the top of the tree.
2. The doctor operated on him quickly, and he was soon out of the woods.
3. Mark takes very good care of his garden because he has green fingers.
4. I don't go by the big brands while shopping; money doesn't grow on trees.
5. Most of these questions are from the unit that I didn't revise, and now I am up a tree.
6. He was barking up the wrong tree so the committee members did not pay any heed to his opinion.

B. Match the idioms with their meanings. Then use any two idioms in sentences of your own.

Column A	Column B
1. up a tree	a. to have gardening skills
2. green fingers	b. out of danger or difficulties
3. top of the tree	c. everything is not easily available
4. out of the woods	d. following a wrong line of thought
5. barking up the wrong tree	e. hold the highest level of a profession
6. money doesn't grow on trees	f. to be in a difficult situation without escape

C. **Complete the rhyming pairs from the poem. Then add two more rhyming words of your own.**

1. street ....
2. most ....
3. gem ....
4. wood ....

ACTIVITY

A. **Conduct a tree survey in your neighbourhood. Then record the findings in the following format.**

- Variety of trees ....
- Number of trees ....
- Most common tree in the locality ....
- Number of trees cut down (within a year) ....
- Reason for cutting down trees ....
- If any new trees were planted in place of the old ones ....
- Any community activities to prevent felling of trees

  ....

  ....

  ....

  ....

- Whether the residents find the removal of trees objectionable

  ....

  ....

  ....

  ....

B. **Present your findings in the class. Note down the information collected about other neighbourhoods. Then, summarise your findings in the following table.**

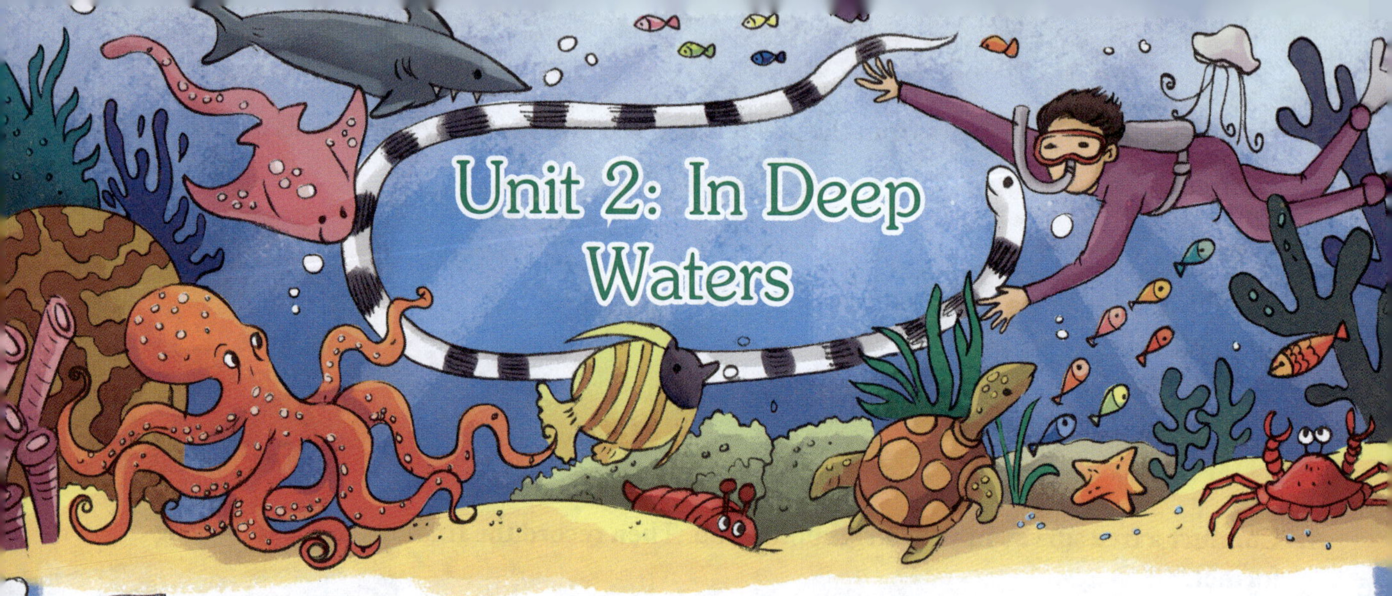

Unit 2: In Deep Waters

WARM-UP

A. Form four groups in the class. Each group should choose any one of the following animal movies. Watch the movies if you haven't already.

- *A Bug's Life*
- *Finding Nemo*
- *Ice Age*
- *The Jungle Book*
- *Finding Dory*
- *Happy Feet*
- *Madagascar*
- *The Lion King*

What did you learn about animals and their life, and their relationship with the environment? What effect do such movies have on the audience? Write down your views and share them with the class.

....

....

....

....

....

B. Imagine you are stranded on an isolated island. Write the names of six things you would need to survive. Discuss why you chose what you did.

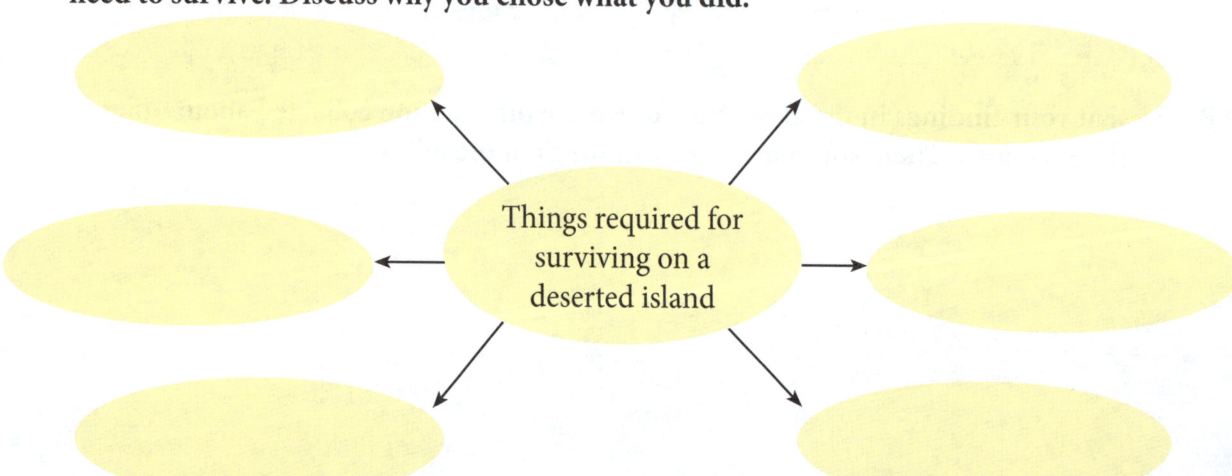

C. **Write the name of your favourite aquatic animal, and then fill in facts about it. Take the help of the Internet or your school library for finding information.**

My favourite aquatic animal is ....

This animal is a

☐ fish ☐ mammal ☐ reptile ☐ other

This animal is found in	This animal eats	This animal's natural enemies are	A fun fact about this animal is ......
....	....	....	....

4 Saving Dory

OBJECTIVES

In this chapter, we will:

- *read the article about marine conservation.*
- *learn words related to conservation, make sentences, and learn about parts of a dictionary entry.*
- *learn the use of simple past tense, adjectives, and the apostrophe.*
- *conduct a mock press conference, and practise short and long e vowel sounds.*
- *write a newspaper article.*

14 LIFE BELOW WATER

READING

Do you like watching films about animals? Read an article on how such films affect the environment and nature.

Do the names Nemo, Dory, Bruce, and Crush ring a bell? They are all characters from the 2016 animated film, *Finding Dory*, the sequel to the 2003 film, *Finding Nemo*.

Finding Nemo follows the journey of Marlin, a clownfish, and Dory, a regal blue tang, all the way to Sydney Harbour to rescue Marlin's son, Nemo, who was stolen from his coral reef home to live out his numbered days in the care of a dentist's niece. *Finding Dory* saw the forgetful blue tang set out on an epic adventure across oceans to find her parents. They are both touching, funny, and inspiring tales that teach us about the beauty of the ocean, its coral reefs, and some of their most attractive inhabitants. People fell in love with the clownfish and the blue regal tang.

sequel: a book or film that continues the story of a previous book or film
regal: royal
epic: grand
inspiring: encouraging or motivating

Though the message of the films are centred on conservation and the tragedy of taking wild coral fish species from their homes and placing them in glass prisons, *Finding Nemo* had a sad and ironic effect too. The clownfish became instantly in-demand pets, causing many more Nemos to be taken from their coral reef ecosystems. *National Geographic* has said that the demand for clownfish as aquarium pets more than tripled as a direct result of the film.

A conservation fund established to protect clownfish, SavingNemo.org, has stated that more than one million clownfish are now taken from coral reef systems each year to go to aquariums, with 400,000 of these fish being sent to the USA. This is causing the fish to go completely extinct in certain areas in south-east Asia.

Clownfish, also known as anemone fish, are found in the Indian and Pacific Oceans. They are usually found living amidst sheltered reefs. Here, they have a symbiotic relationship with sea anemones, a marine predatory animal which looks like a beautiful flower. They protect each other from predators and exchange nutrients. The clownfish even cleans the anemone! In return, the anemone keeps its harpoon-like stingers, used to capture prey and scare predators, at bay from the clownfish.

In an amazing feat of nature, these fish develop into males first, and become females as mature fish in order to reproduce. They lay their eggs on flat surfaces near their anemone hosts.

Science Scan

- The regal blue tang is also known as blue surgeonfish, common surgeon, or doctorfish. This is because they have sharp, poisonous spine which is shaped like a scalpel (the sharp knife used by surgeons).
- There are 28 different species of clownfish, which come in many colours, such as pink, red, yellow, black, brown, and multi-coloured stripes.
- All clownfish are born male and can turn into females. But they cannot go back to being males once this change is made.

The regal blue tang is found in the waters off East Africa to the central Pacific island of Kiribati, as well as around Japan and Australia. They too like to live in the coral reefs that grow along the sea shore. When they see a predator, they often 'play dead' by lying on their side and staying motionless till the creature passes them by.

The blue tang is very important to the life cycle of the coral reef, as they eat the excess algae in the reef, thus preventing the algae to suffocate the reef. They use their small, sharp teeth to keep their coral protectors clean.

Interestingly, *Finding Dory* shows Dory's parents as kind and nurturing. In real life, however, the parents don't care for their young. Baby blue tangs are carried away by ocean currents soon after they hatch, and are on their own from the very beginning. On the other hand, clownfish dads do watch over their eggs and fan them, which keep the anemones clean, and take care of the eggs.

ironic: happening in a way that is opposite to what is expected

symbiotic: a relationship between organisms, people, or things that exist together and depend on each other, that benefits them all

predatory: animals that live by killing other animals for food

harpoon: (here) like the long sharp spear

feat: (here) an achievement

These fish species aren't the first glamour pets to rise to popularity due to Hollywood films, and to suffer because of it. Do you remember the Snowy Owl, Hedwig, in the *Harry Potter* films? The boy wizard's love for his pet sparked an increase in the demand for owls as pets in many countries. But many of the birds ended up in animal shelters soon after the series ended. Moreover, owls are illegal to own, without suitable qualifications, in many countries.

The popularity of the *Teenage Mutant Ninja Turtles*, a series of comic book-based films about a group of pizza-loving, stunt-performing turtles, saw a huge increase in turtles as pets. But many of them were abandoned and even flushed away when their owners got bored.

How do films that celebrate a love of ocean creatures and convey a strong conservation message leave us with a crisis of this nature? We only have our greed to own beautiful possessions to blame for it. If we love and admire these fish and other marine creatures, we should raise awareness about their condition. The message of the films, and now the science, is clear: *just let them keep swimming in the ocean.*

Science Scan

- Turtles and tortoises are both reptiles; but the former lives in water and the latter on land.
- Turtles have light-weight shells and have webbed feet with long claws; tortoises have heavier shells, and have short, bent legs.

abandoned: given up or forsaken
crisis: a time of great danger or trouble
techniques: methods of doing certain activities
anaesthetic: a substance that makes you unconscious and unable to feel pain
bred: animals kept for producing offspring in a controlled manner
captivity: imprisoned; in a state of confinement
fragile: delicate; something that can be easily damaged

But marine fish harvesting techniques can be careless and cruel. Many of these bright blue and yellow-coloured fish die before they make it to someone's living room. Often, cyanide poisoning is used on reefs to harvest the fish. Cyanide acts as an anaesthetic that allows fish to be collected faster and more easily.

Another impact of *Finding Nemo* was that some aquarium owners who kept clownfish saw the film and felt so bad that they released their pets into the wild. Many people also bought the clownfish without knowing how to take care of them. Perhaps led on by a line in the film, many children are said to have flushed their clownfish down the toilet in the hope of setting them free. Often, the clownfish could not survive in the new oceanic ecosystems that they were not used to. They also sometimes harmed the local fish there as introduced pests.

When *Finding Dory* was released in 2016, marine scientists had a clear message: Don't let it happen to Dory. The regal blue tang—which, unlike the clownfish, cannot be bred in captivity—could suffer the same fate.

Around 300,000 blue tangs are bought and sold across the world. But regal blue tangs do not do well in aquariums. They are fragile and require specialised care, and in the wrong circumstances, die in large numbers.

SUMMARY

This factual article is about how animal films can deeply affect nature and its diverse inhabitants. The film *Finding Nemo* traces the journey of a clownfish named Marlin, and a blue tang called Dory, all the way to Sydney Harbour to save Marlin's son Nemo. Nemo was stolen from his home to live in the care of a dentist's niece. Similarly, *Finding Dory* witnesses the blue tang setting out on an adventure across oceans to find her parents. Though the message of these films was about marine conservation, after watching *Finding Nemo*, the demand for clownfish increased, ironically resulting in more such fishes been taken from their coral reef ecosystems.

COMPREHENSION

A. Read the lines from the article and answer the questions.

1. *They are both touching, funny, and inspiring tales.*
   a. Name the two tales.
   b. What type of animals the tales are based on?
   c. What was the initial reaction of the audience?
2. *When they see a predator, they often 'play dead'...*
   a. Who does 'they' refer to?
   b. Explain the phrase 'play dead'.
   c. Why are 'they' very important for the life cycle of the coral reef?
3. *In an amazing feat of nature, these fish develop into males first.*
   a. Name 'these fish'.
   b. What can they turn into? Why?
   c. Name the conservation fund that has been established to protect these fish.
4. *We only have our greed to own beautiful possessions to blame for it.*
   a. Who does 'we' refer to?
   b. What are 'we' to be blamed for?
   c. How can 'we' help to protect marine life?

B. Answer these questions briefly.

1. What was the animation film *Finding Nemo* about?
2. What unforeseen negative effect did the film have?
3. Explain the symbiotic relationship that exists between the clownfish and the sea anemones.
4. How are clownfish dads different from regal blue tang parents?
5. Why is an aquarium not suitable for a regal blue tang?
6. What was the fate of the turtles which were bought as pets after the popularity of the *Teenage Mutant Ninja Turtles?*
7. How are marine fish harvesting techniques careless and cruel?
8. The article mentions a glamour bird pet. What do you know about it? Write in your own words.

C. Complete the following diagram with information about the situation of clownfish and the regal blue tang.

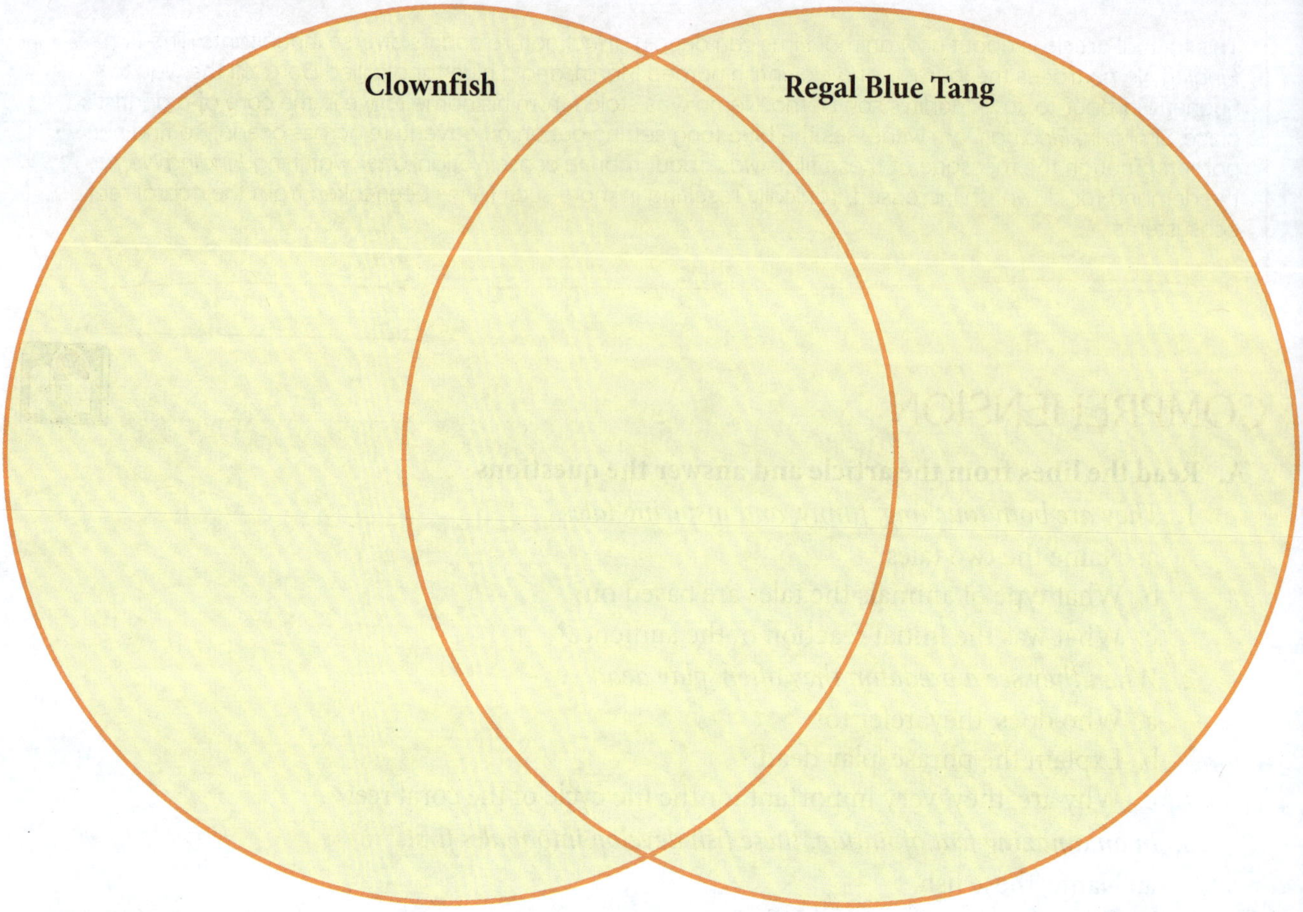

Life Skills and Values

Sensitivity towards animals

1. Do you think that filmmakers, who have animals as their main characters, should be more conscious about the message that gets delivered through their films? Support your answer with relevant points from the article.
2. *Animals should not be kept as pets.* What is your opinion about this statement?

VOCABULARY

A. Find words related to conservation in the word grid. One has been done for you.

~~care~~ *control* *fortify* *maintain* *nurture* *protect* *provide* *safeguard* *shelter* *shield* *sustain*

P	R	O	T	E	C	T	A	B	L	C	M	E	D	F	D
G	Z	Z	T	Y	Z	A	D	F	O	S	A	F	R	V	A
H	Y	X	R	U	D	S	R	G	R	A	I	G	A	U	N
I	X	C	W	L	X	E	S	H	T	P	N	H	U	T	U
J	W	V	E	I	T	D	A	J	N	O	T	J	G	S	R
K	V	I	Q	L	C	F	Q	L	O	I	A	K	E	R	T
L	H	B	E	P	V	G	W	M	C	U	I	L	F	Q	U
S	U	H	A	L	B	H	E	N	D	Y	N	P	A	P	R
M	S	N	E	K	N	J	R	B	F	T	D	O	S	O	E
F	T	E	V	R	E	S	E	R	P	R	S	I	W	N	B
O	S	M	S	J	M	K	T	V	G	E	A	U	X	M	C
R	R	L	D	H	A	L	Y	C	H	W	C	Y	Y	L	D
T	Q	K	P	R	O	V	I	D	E	Q	Z	A	Z	K	E
I	P	J	F	G	S	I	U	X	J	M	X	T	R	J	F
F	O	H	G	F	D	P	O	Z	K	N	C	R	Q	E	G
Y	N	S	U	S	T	A	I	N	L	B	V	E	W	I	H

B. Make sentences of your own using these words.

1. aquarium 2. feat 3. fragile 4. predator 5. turtle

DICTIONARY SKILLS

Parts of a Dictionary Entry

pronunciation key — plural — word — meanings — part of speech; grammar — example sentence

ancillary

an|ces/tor/ænsestə^{r}/ **(ancestors)** [1] Your **ancestors** are the people from whom you are descended. ☐*...our daily lives, so different from those of our ancestors... He could trace his ancestors back seven hundred years.* [2] An **ancestor of** something modern is an earlier thing from which it developed. ☐ *The direct ancestor of the modern cat was the Kaffir cat of ancient Egypt.*

N-COUNT; usu pl, with poss ≠ *descendant*

N-COUNT; usu N *of* n ≠ *descendant*

Find the meanings of these words using a dictionary. Identify the part of speech. Then, make sentences using each word.

1. beast
2. valiant
3. dismal
4. ghastly
5. cowards
6. fabulous

GRAMMAR

Simple Past Tense

We use the **simple past tense** to describe an action that has already happened before, and is no longer happening.

- In regular verbs, the past tense is formed by adding *d* or *-ed* to the verbs.

  love → loved *enjoy → enjoyed*

- In verbs with a single vowel followed by a consonant, the past tense is usually formed by doubling the final consonant and adding *-ed* to it. For example:

  plan → planned *stop → stopped*

- Many verbs are irregular and the past tense is different from the base verb. For example:

  be → was *come → came* *do → did* *have → had*

  know → knew *sing → sang* *tell → told* *write → wrote*

- The verb form in both regular and irregular verbs are same for all persons (*I, you, she, he, it, we, they*) in the past tense. For example:

  Sana fell in love with her baby brother the moment she saw him.

A. Fill in the blanks with the simple past tense form of the verbs in brackets.

1. My father .... (*buy*) a pet dog for us last month.
2. Last week I .... (*go*) to the museum with my parents.
3. He .... (*pay*) the bill on time to avoid being a defaulter.
4. The Ray siblings .... (*visit*) their grandparents last week.
5. The teacher .... (*tell*) us to complete the project in the class.
6. He .... (*bring*) a box of chocolates to school for his friends.
7. My brother .... (*cut*) the cake last evening as it was his birthday.
8. As soon as Rahul opened the cage, the bird .... (*fly*) away.
9. We .... (*stay*) near the beach when we went to Puducherry.
10. We .... (*write*) to the authorities regarding frequent power cuts.

Adjectives

- An **adjective** is a word that describes and provides more information about a noun or a pronoun.
- Adjectives describe features (size, shape, age, or colour) of people, animals, and things. For example:

  I gave my mother beautiful, long-stemmed, pink roses for her birthday.
- Adjectives can express the kind or quality of a thing or a person. For example:

  Marine fish harvesting techniques can be careless and cruel.

  The forgetful blue tang set out on an epic adventure across oceans to find her parents.

B. Underline the adjectives in each sentence.

1. It was a cloudy and windy day.
2. London has extremely cold and wet winters.
3. I read a long and interesting adventure novel.
4. We must always keep our surroundings clean.
5. My grandmother bakes delicious cakes and puddings.
6. Ravi is loved by all because he is kind and helpful.
7. Our new home may be small, but it is airy and comfortable.
8. The last house on our block belongs to the police commissioner.

Apostrophe

- An **apostrophe** is a punctuation mark (') used to indicate either contraction or possession.
- In contractions, it is written to indicate that one or more letters have been left out. For example:

do not → don't	*it is → it's*	*is not → isn't*
you have → you've	*cannot → can't*	*will not → won't*

  wh word + *'s/'d → what's (what is/has); who'd (who had/who would)*
- An apostrophe can be added to nouns to show possession or belonging. For example:

  noun + 's → This is Rohan's bat. *This is Mike's car.*

C. Rewrite the following sentences using the apostrophe wherever required.

1. I cannot go out to play as it is raining.
2. They are going for a picnic on Sunday.
3. The young boy does not know his way home.
4. The dress that belongs to Neha is very colourful.
5. The desk that belonged to the author was scattered with books.
6. The tennis racket which belonged to Pooja was taken by her younger sister.
7. Do you think he will go home after the match?
8. The ring tone of the phone is loud and annoying.

LISTENING AND SPEAKING

Listening

A. Listen to the passage and fill in the blanks.

1. The Marine National Park is located on the .... shore of the .... of Kutch.
2. It has .... islands on the .... coast.
3. Some of the flora and fauna which can be seen in the park are coral ...., sea ...., painted ...., shelled molluscs, and ....
4. The national park is the first .... wildlife sanctuary and the first .... national park in India.

Speaking

21st CENTURY SKILLS Collaboration

B. Imagine there is an urgent need to understand a fragile ecosystem and preserve an endangered species. Organise a mock press conference in the class. Divide the class into three groups. One group will represent the conservation committee, another the scientists, and the third the media. The media will ask questions directed towards the conservation committee or the scientists. Role-play the interview.

Pronunciation

C. Adding an *-e* at the end of a word often changes the short vowel sound to a long vowel sound. Add *-e* to the following words to make new words with a long vowel sound. Then say them aloud.

1. bit......	3. gap......	5. hop......	7. sit......
2. cap......	4. hat......	6. pan......	8. tap......

WRITING

Write a newspaper article on an imaginary incident about an exotic fish being seen in the sea. Include these points.

- Where was it first seen?
- What time of the year was it?
- What did it look like?
- What was the reaction of the onlookers?
- Where did the fish end up—aquarium or the sea?
- Who made the decision? What led to this decision?

5 The Man on the Island

–Robert Louis Stevenson

OBJECTIVES

In this chapter, we will:

- *read the extract from the adventure novel Treasure Island.*
- *solve a crossword related to sailing, and learn collocations.*
- *learn the order of adjectives and use of articles.*
- *listen and identify information as true or false; enact a conversation to express views, and learn about word stress.*
- *write an email.*

READING

Squire Trelawney is a nobleman in the village. When Jim Hawkins discovers a treasure map which belonged to a pirate, Trelawney had the means to hire a ship and take Jim and Dr Livesey, the local doctor, on a real-life treasure hunt. Read on to find out what happens when Jim reaches the island and realises that someone is following him.

Some stones came rolling down the side of the hill. Somebody was up there, among the trees! I saw a figure run from one tree to the next. It was a strange figure. Dark and hairy it was. Was it a man or a monkey? Was it a wild man? I fled.

The creature followed me. On and on I ran. The creature was never far away. As fast as a hare it ran, its body bent almost double. But it moved, like a man, on two legs. 'If it is a man, why am I afraid?' I asked myself. 'I have my pistol.'

I stopped running. I took my pistol from my belt and walked towards the creature. It came out from behind a tree trunk, moved two or three steps towards me, and then stopped. It was a man!

He threw himself on his knees in front of me. He clasped his hands and held them out to me. He seemed to be begging for mercy!

'Who are you?' I asked.

'Ben Gunn. I'm poor Ben Gunn. I've lived here, all alone these three years. Three years—all by myself!'

He was a white man like myself but he had been burned black by the sun. His blue eyes looked strange in his dark face. His hair and beard were long and snow-white. His clothes were rags, held together by string or sticks.

'Three years!' I cried. 'Were you shipwrecked?'

'No. I was marooned.'

I began to feel very sorry for the poor fellow. Marooned! Left here alone by the pirates. Left here to die slowly of hunger although he had managed, somehow, to live on!

'Marooned,' repeated Ben Gunn. 'Three years ago. I've lived on wild goats, berries, and shellfish. Ah! Wouldn't I like some proper food! You don't happen to have any cheese with you? Night after night, I've dreamt of cheese. What wouldn't I give for just a taste!'

'I'm sorry,' I said, 'I don't happen to have any cheese with me. But, if I get on board again, you shall have all the cheese you can eat.'

Ben Gunn had been fingering the cloth of my coat and stroking my hands. He stopped suddenly and asked sharply, 'Who's stopping you from going on board?'

'Not you, I know,' I answered.

'Ah, no, not I... What's your name, my lad?'

'Jim.'

'Jim, Jim,' he repeated. Then, in a rush, he told me: 'Well, Jim, I've been living a rough life. But I was carefully brought up. My mother was a good woman, Jim. She taught me to say my prayers... then I went wrong. And that brought me here. But I've been thinking. If ever I get off this island, I'm going to lead a good life. A good, holy life, Jim.'

clasped: held tightly or firmly
mercy: (here) kindness, forgiveness
shipwrecked: experienced a shipwreck; being part of an accident at sea in which a ship is destroyed
marooned: left behind or stranded in a place from where one cannot escape
pirates: sailors who attack and rob other ships at sea
fingering: touching or handling with the fingers

He stopped for breath. Then he whispered in my ear, 'I'm rich, Jim! I'm rich!'

I was thinking that the poor fellow was mad. His loneliness must have made him mad.

Perhaps he read my thoughts, for he said, angrily, 'You don't believe me... but it's true. You were the first that found me, Jim, and I'll give you a share.'

A frightened look came over his face. 'Jim,' he said, 'tell me the truth. You're not on Flint's ship, are you?'

I answered him readily for I felt that he was a friend.

'No, it's not Flint's ship. Flint is dead. But some of his men are on the ship, and that's bad for us.' 'Is there... is there a man with one leg?'

'Long John Silver?'

'Ay! That's his name.'

'He's there. He's the cook and he's the leader of Flint's men.'

All this time, Ben Gunn had been holding my hand. Now, he pressed it so hard that I almost cried out. 'You haven't come from Long John, have you? Tell me the truth, lad! If he's sent you, then it's the end of Ben Gunn.'

I decided to tell him the whole story of our voyage and our present danger. I did so. He listened with great interest. When I had finished, he stroked my hand. 'You're a good lad, Jim,' he said. 'You're in a nasty corner but we'll find a way out. Trust in Ben Gunn. Ben Gunn is the man. I'll help you, Jim.'

He paused a moment. Then he asked me, 'Tell me, Jim, is your Mr Trelawney likely to be generous to a man who helped him?'

'The Squire's a gentleman,' I said, 'and a generous man as well.'

'Do you think that he'd let me have—say—a thousand pounds of the money—the money that's mine already?'

'I'm sure he would. He's promised all the men a fair share.'

'And my passage home as well?'

'Of course. We'll need you to help us sail the ship home.'

'That's true,' he said, looking pleased. 'So you will.'

He stroked my hand. Then he said, 'Well, Jim, you've told me your story. Now, I'll tell you mine. I was on Flint's ship when he came here with the treasure. Billy Bones was the mate. Long John was in charge of the stores. Flint went on shore with six of the men. Big, strong fellows they were. After a week, he came back on board, alone. He'd buried the treasure—and killed the six fellows. He sailed away at once. Then, it happened that, three years ago, I was on another ship and we saw this island. 'That's Flint's island,' I told my mates. 'Let's go and look for his treasure.' We looked for it for twelve days but we didn't find it. My shipmates were very angry with me. 'Here, Benjamin,' they said, 'here's a gun and an axe. We're leaving you here to find Flint's treasure.' They sailed away and left me here.'

ay: an archaic word for *yes*
voyage: a long journey on a ship
nasty corner: a bad or unpleasant situation
a way out: deal with the problem
generous: willing to help or give money, especially more than is usual or expected
Squire: (in former times) a landowner, with a high social rank, in an English village
passage: trip; a journey by ship
mate: the person who is second in command of a ship after the captain
in charge of: having responsibility for

Ben Gunn stopped and asked me anxiously, 'You'll speak to Mr Trelawney for me, Jim, won't you?'

'Yes,' I promised him. 'But I don't know how I'm going to get back on board.'

'You can have my boat, Jim. I made it myself, with my own two hands. It's lying there, just under the White Rock.'

At that moment, we heard the sound of the ship's cannon—two hours before sunset!

'They're fighting!' I cried. 'Come on, Ben!'

We jumped up and ran in the direction of the Bay. The cannon had stopped but guns were being fired. The fight had begun. We ran on in the direction of the ship.

I stopped suddenly. High above some trees, the English flag was flying.

'Your friends are there, Jim. You go on. I shan't come with you. If Mr Trelawney or the other gentlemen want to see me, you know where to find me,' Ben Gunn told me.

'Thank you, Ben,' I said, running fast towards the flag.

anxiously: worriedly
cannon: a large gun, usually on wheels, and used in battles

SUMMARY

In this extract from *Treasure Island*, Jim Hawkins reaches the island on a real-life treasure hunt. Initially he feels that a strange creature is following him, but soon he discovers that it is a man named Ben Gunn. The latter tells Jim how he was marooned on the island by his shipmates because he had told them about the treasure hidden on the island by a man named Flint. However, they didn't find anything when they searched the place. Ben agrees to share the treasure with Jim if the latter gets the Squire to help him. Jim does not know how to get back on board, so Ben offers him the boat that he had made. Luckily, Jim's ship returns to take him back.

About the Author

Robert Louis Stevenson (1850–1894) was a famous Scottish novelist, travel writer, and poet. His most famous works include *Treasure Island, Kidnapped, Strange Case of Dr Jekyll and Mr Hyde, The Black Arrow*, and *A Child's Garden of Verses*. Stevenson travelled extensively through the Pacific islands of Hawaii, Kiribati, Tahiti, and Samoa. He eventually settled down in Upolo, an island in Samoa, and took the Samoan name *Tusitala* meaning a storyteller. He was loved by the Samoans, and when he died, the inscription on his tombstone was translated into a Samoan song of grief.

COMPREHENSION

A. Complete these sentences.

1. .... was marooned on the island for .... years.
2. The man on the island asked Jim for some ....
3. Flint buried the .... and killed the ....

4. The .... had stopped but guns were being fired.
5. High above some trees, the .... was flying.

B. Answer these questions briefly.

1. Why did Jim think that there was someone atop the hill, among the trees?
2. Describe the man whom Jim came across on the island.
3. How did the man on the island come to be there?
4. What food item did Ben ask Jim for, and why?

C. Think and answer the questions.

1. Do you think that Ben Gunn had found the hidden treasure? Support your answer with evidence from the story.
2. Why do you think Ben decided not to go with Jim to the ship?

Life Skills and Values

Presence of mind

1. What would you do if you were faced with a similar situation as Jim in the story?
2. Imagine you found a hidden treasure. What would you do with it? On what basis would you decide? Share your reasoning.

VOCABULARY

A. Read the clues and solve the crossword puzzle.

Across

2. a voyage on a ship for pleasure
4. drifting about
5. a person who robs ships at sea
7. be overturned in water

Down

1. come into a harbour
3. captain of the ship
4. an exciting experience
6. a call used by sailors

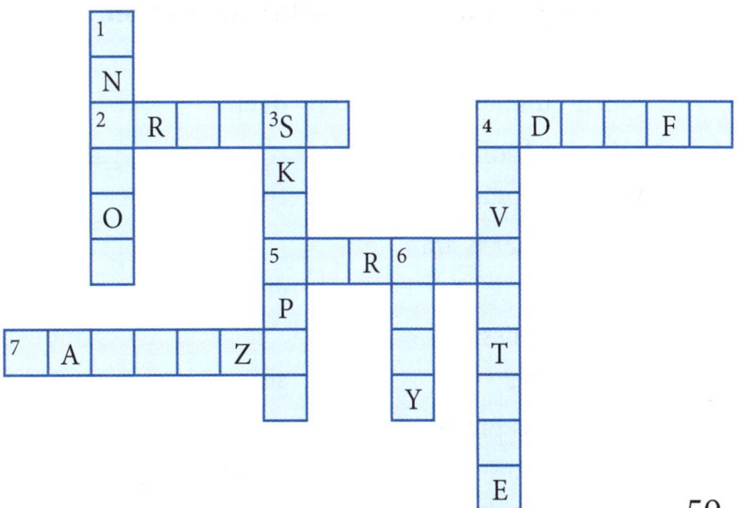

Collocations

- A **collocation** is a combination of two or more words that are generally used together as a whole in a way that sounds naturally correct.
- A collocation can be a combination of *verb + noun*. For example:

verb	noun
read / write / send / delete	*an email*
take / pass / fail	*an exam*

- A collocation can be a combination of *adjective + noun*. For example:

adjective	noun
mild	*climate / curry / winter*
soft	*drink / light / music*

- In the phrase *a mild curry, mild* is the collocation for *curry*. Here we cannot use the words *mellow* or *gentle*, even though they are synonyms of *mild* because it does not sound correct.

B. Use the verb *make* or *do* to complete these collocations.

1. .... a favour
2. .... a mess
3. .... a point
4. .... friends
5. .... good
6. .... read
7. .... laundry
8. .... a noise
9. .... progress
10. .... sense
11. .... something right
12. .... your homework

C. The following sentences contain an incomplete adjective-noun collocation. Choose the correct option and complete the collocation.

1. The sisters share a .... bond of affection.
   a. bottomless b. deep c. heavy
2. We need some .... air in this stuffy room.
   a. additional b. fresh c. new
3. My brother is a/an .... admirer of Albert Einstein.
   a. ardent b. enthusiastic c. keen
4. Do not miss the .... opportunity or you will regret it.
   a. golden b. shiny c. silver
5. Mr Roy is proud of his .... possession, a brand-new watch.
   a. latest b. modern c. up-to-date

Order of Adjectives

- When more than one adjective describes a noun, the adjectives must follow a certain sequence. This sequence is known as the **order of adjectives** and is as follows:

Opinion	Physical Description				Origin	Material	Qualifier	Noun
	Size	Shape	Age	Colour				
beautiful			*old*			*wooden*	*hat*	*boxes*
delicious					*Thai*			*food*
	huge				*Japanese*		*Sumo*	*wrestlers*
expensive			*antique*			*silver*		*mirrors*
famous					*Russian*		*touring*	*circus*
gorgeous		*long-stemmed*		*red*		*silk*		*roses*

- Notice that first the opinion or observation is made, followed by its physical description.
- The physical description also follows a specific order (size, shape, age, and colour).
- This is followed by the origin, material, and qualifier.

A. Put a tick (✓) against the group of adjectives that are in the correct order and a cross (✗) against those that are incorrect. Rewrite the correct order in the blanks.

1. a blue big bag ☐ ....
2. short black hair ☐ ....
3. a funny little boy ☐ ....
4. a brown coffee cup ☐ ....
5. a/an old lovely vase ☐ ....
6. the first five months ☐ ....
7. a brown leather folder ☐ ....
8. the three last chapters ☐ ....
9. a big old English sheepdog ☐ ....
10. a serving tray small Mexican ☐ ....
11. a/an beautiful old Italian touring van ☐ ....
12. a massive square brick-red office building ☐ ....

Articles

- **Articles** indicate whether a noun is specific or general.
- There are two types of articles—indefinite and definite articles.

Indefinite article

- The **indefinite article** is *a* or *an*. It is used for non-specific nouns, or when we do not specify the things or people we are talking about. It is also always used with a singular noun. For example:

  It was a strange figure.

  They gave Benjamin an axe.

Definite article

- The **definite article** is *the*. It is used when we talk about a specific thing that both the speaker and the listener know. For example:

  The creature followed me.

  Flint buried the treasure.

Some rules

- When we speak of someone or something for the first time, we use *a* or *an*. The next time we repeat that noun, we use *the*. For example:

  It was a strange figure. The creature followed me.

- The indefinite article *a* is placed before words that begin with a consonant sound, while the indefinite article *an* is always placed before words that begin with a vowel sound. For example:

  a creature

  an island

B. Fill in the blanks with suitable articles.

1. It was .... beautiful painting.
2. Do not lean against .... wall.
3. My brother is .... honest boy.
4. I ate .... apple in the morning.
5. It was pouring cats and dogs, so I carried .... umbrella.
6. While returning home, I came across .... beggar.
7. My family decided to visit .... museum on Sunday.
8. Fatima was reading .... book when the doorbell rang.
9. .... lion is .... king of .... jungle.
10. David Livingstone was .... famous Scottish missionary and .... explorer.

LISTENING AND SPEAKING

Listening

A. Listen to the passage carefully and mark the sentences as true (T) or false (F).

1. The author of *Treasure Island* is Squire Trelawney. ☐
2. Jim's father owned the Admiral Benbow Inn. ☐
3. The captain had a white scar across one cheek. ☐
4. He offered Jim a gold coin for his services. ☐
5. All day long he hung around the cove or sat on the cliffs. ☐

Speaking

B. Enact a conversation between a pirate and a sailor who are sharing their individual experiences with each other. At the end of the conversation, discuss and decide which of them has a more adventurous life.

Pronunciation

Word stress

In English, we do not say each syllable with the same weight. Each syllable in a word can be stressed or unstressed. The emphasis that we place in a specific syllable of a word pronunciation, is known as **word stress**. For example:

AC.tion *AN.swer*

FU.ture *GA.rden*

- In the above words, the stress is on the first syllable (the letters in capital).

ad.VANTAGE *ex.AMPLE*

em.BRACE *re.VISION*

- In the above words, the stress falls after the first syllable (the letters in capital).
- The dot (.) in each word divides the words into syllables.

C. Say the words aloud. They have been broken into syllables. Underline the syllable where you think the word stress falls.

1. a.nother
2. boul.der
3. ca.rrot
4. de.lay
5. em.press
6. fee.ling
7. ho.nest
8. mo.ment
9. to.day
10. to.night

WRITING

Emails are similar to letters. They can be formal or informal. Keep these points in mind while writing an email:

- Every email has an email address.
- When addressing the email to several people, fill in the cc/bcc column.
- The salutation includes the first name of the addressee or an appropriate form of address.
- The mail ends with a proper subscription followed by your name, just as in a letter.

New Message

Send | Attach | Address | Fonts | Colours | Save As Draft

To: smriti@abc.in

Cc:

Subject: My first plane journey

Signature: Signature #1

Dear Smriti,

I hope you are doing well. I am writing to share with you my first aeroplane journey from New Delhi to Mumbai. I was excited but scared as well.

My mother helped me to get the boarding pass. I got my bag checked-in and waited for the boarding call. Then it was time to board the flight. After boarding, I sat with my mother and fastened the seat belt. As the engines roared, I got very scared. I held my mother's hand and closed my eyes. After ten minutes, we were in the air. I enjoyed the view from the top and felt elated. After two hours, we landed in Mumbai, and my fear was gone.

It was a great flight, and my first plane journey will always be memorable.

Give my regards to your parents, and write to me soon.

Yours lovingly,

Palak

Your uncle is an explorer. You accompanied him on a submarine to search for a hidden treasure in the Indian Ocean. Write an email to your friend describing the experience. Cover the following points in your email.

21st Century Skills: Creative Thinking

- Feelings on boarding a submarine for the first time (fear, excitement, or curiosity)
- Expectations
- Any responsibility undertaken by you

6 Upon the Songs of Whales

–Cori MacNaughton

OBJECTIVES

In this chapter, we will:
- *read the poem about marine life.*
- *learn about alliteration and rhyme scheme.*
- *read and write a limerick.*

14 LIFE BELOW WATER

READING

Did you know that blue whales and humpback whales sing? The different kinds of whales make different sounds and together they create harmony in the sea.

The finest singer in the sea
I heard upon this morn
And in that strange, sonorous tone
A universe was born.

The low melodic wailing touched
And roused me from my sleep
As the humpback lithe and languid
Made a turn and sounded deep.

humpback: a large whale with a raised area known as a hump and long flippers
sonorous: deep, ringing, and pleasant sound; (here) deeply musical
wailing: crying loudly with anger, pain, or sadness
roused: awakened
lithe: able to move and bend easily and gracefully; flexible
languid: moved slowly in a lazy manner

Fact File

- Whale songs are thought to be a form of communication between whales. They can be heard many kilometers away and for several hours or days.
- While the bigger whales create deep melodious sounds like songs, the smaller toothed whales make high-pitched whistling and clicking sounds.

Literary Device

To the snowy white beluga
The canary of them all.
This is an example of a **metaphor** which compares two different things with something in common. Here the snow-white beluga is compared to a bright yellow canary bird because of its beautiful voice.

beluga: a small white whale with a bulbous head found in the Arctic coastal regions
sperm whale: a large whale with an enormous head and the largest brain on Earth
California grey: a whale that looks like a crusty ocean rock as it is usually covered with parasites
pilot whale: a whale with black skin and a bulbous head found in all seas except polar seas
complex: complicated
orcas: large-toothed whales with black-and-white markings that hunt in groups
dialects: forms of a language spoken in different parts of a place, or by a specific group
awful: extremely shocking
glee: happiness and excitement

And as my mind awakes it turns
To whales large and small
To the snowy white beluga
The canary of them all.

The clicking bursts of sperm whales
And the California grey
The fin whale speaks across the sea
To those a world away.

The short and long-finned pilot whales
With whistles quite complex
The striking graceful orcas
Speak in different dialects.

But it is the great blue whale
That makes the loudest cry
Though it is far too rare today
With such an awful why.

But on this wondrous morning I
Am filled with joyous glee
That God has given life to whales
And gave to them the sea.

SUMMARY

The poem talks about different kinds of whales and the variety of sounds that they produce. According to the poet, the various sounds made by the whales create a kind of harmony in the sea. The poet is awakened from her sleep by the wailing sound made by the humpback. The beluga is compared to a canary because both have beautiful voices. Other different sounds are made by the sperm whales, pilot whales, and orcas among others. The poem ends on a happy note as the whales continue to inhabit the sea and produce a beautiful melody in the ocean.

About the Poet

Cori MacNaughton is a longtime writer, researcher, artist, poet, musician and occasional voiceover artist. Her works lay emphasis on the natural world and its diverse inhabitants, land use and water rights, agriculture and green living in general. She is fascinated by rare plants, and loves farming and gardening organically.

COMPREHENSION

A. Choose the correct option.

1. The song of the whales
   a. woke the poet from sleep.
   b. was heard by the poet at night.
   c. disturbed her as she was studying.
2. The blue whale is known for its
   a. whistles.
   b. loud cry.
   c. clicking bursts.
3. The low melodic wailing was produced by the
   a. orca.
   b. beluga whale.
   c. humpback whale.

B. Read the lines from the poem and answer the questions.

1. *The finest singer in the sea*
   I heard upon this morn
   a. Who does the poet refer to as the *finest singer*?
   b. When does the poet hear the song?
2. *Though it is far too rare today*
   With such an awful why.
   a. What does 'it' refer to?
   b. What does the poet mean by 'an awful why'?

C. Answer the questions briefly.

1. Why does the poet say *a universe was born*?
2. How does the melodic wailing of the whales affect the poet?
3. Why do you think the poet refers to the blue whale as a rare animal?

Life Skills and Values

Marine conservation

1. Whales are hunted for their oil, meat, or whalebone. Although it is now banned in several parts of the world, fishermen in certain countries wish to lift this ban. Do you think this ban should be lifted? Give reasons for your answer.
2. How can one contribute towards the preservation of marine life? Share your ideas.

VOCABULARY

Alliteration

- **Alliteration** is a literary device that uses repetition of the same letter or sound at the beginning of words that have been placed together closely. For example:

  My mother made a mango mousse.

- It is usually used in poetry to create a musical rhythm. For example:

  Three grey geese in a green field grazing,
  Grey were the geese and green was the grazing.

- Alliteration is also used to make tongue-twisters. For example:

  Peter Piper picked a peck of pickled peppers.
  Silly Sally swiftly shooed seven silly sheep.

A. Find two examples of alliteration in the poem.

Rhyme Scheme

- A **rhyme scheme** is a regular pattern of rhyme at the end of each line or stanza in a poem.
- It is shown by writing the same letter of the alphabet against the lines which rhyme together.
- There are various kinds of rhyme schemes.
- In the alternate rhyme scheme, the first line rhymes with the third line, whereas the second line rhymes with the fourth line. It is represented as *ABAB*. For example:

  The people along the sand (A)
  All turn and look one way. (B)
  They turn their back on the land. (A)
  They look at the sea all day. (B)

- In the enclosed rhyme scheme, the first and fourth lines rhyme while the second and third lines rhyme. It is represented as *ABBA*. For example:

  Butterfly, butterfly, flutter around, (A)
  Butterfly, butterfly, hop over the tree. (B)
  Butterfly, butterfly, fly so free, (B)
  Butterfly, butterfly, touch the ground. (A)

B. Find out the rhyme scheme of the poem.

ACTIVITY

Limerick

- A **limerick** is a humorous five-line poem.
- It has a rhyme scheme of *AABBA* where the first, second and fifth lines rhyme, while the third and fourth lines rhyme together. All lines must have five to seven syllables. For example:

  There was an Old Man with a beard (A)
  Who said, 'It is just as I feared! (A)
  Two Owls and a Hen, (B)
  Four Larks and a Wren, (B)
  Have all built their nests in my beard!' (A)

Read this limerick. Then, work in pairs and write a limerick on anything you find humorous in nature.

The Genial Grimalkin*

There was an old Cat named Macduff
Who could joke till you cried, 'Hold, enough!'
His Wife and his Child so persistently smiled
That their cheeks got a permanent puff.

*an old Cat

PROJECT 1

14 LIFE BELOW WATER

21st Century Skills — Critical Thinking

Saving Marine Life

Plastic pollution is one of the most common but serious problems in the world, and humans are responsible for it. Plastic debris that floats in the water is ingested by fish, seabirds and marine mammals, and it eventually kills them.

In 2010, a California grey whale died on the shores of the Puget Sound along the northwestern coast of the US. When the whale was examined, a large amount of trash was found in its stomach. The trash included more than 20 plastic bags, a pair of pants, small towels, duct tape, and a golf ball. In June 2018, a female blue whale died from a ship strike on the north of San Francisco. Blue whales are an endangered species, and the death of the largest animal on Earth because of our carelessness is a cause of great concern.

The irresponsible actions of human beings have an adverse affect on marine life. Therefore, a change in lifestyle must be adopted. We should prevent the generation of disposable products, and reduce, recycle, and reuse waste materials.

Think about some ways in which we can protect the marine life. Share your ideas with the class.

In the poem *Upon the Songs of Whales*, the poet has written about seven different types of whales. Form seven groups in your class. Read and research about one whale each and create an information booklet about the whale. You can cover the following points:

- Their habitats
- Distinct characteristics
- Interesting facts

Unit 3: The Differently Abled

WARM-UP

A. There are many people, who, despite being physically challenged, have overcome their disabilities to achieve great success in life. Look at these pictures of some famous achievers. Match them with their professions.

music composer and lyricist *actress and dancer* *German composer and pianist* *painter* *theoretical physicist and cosmologist* *IAS officer*

1. Beethoven

....

....

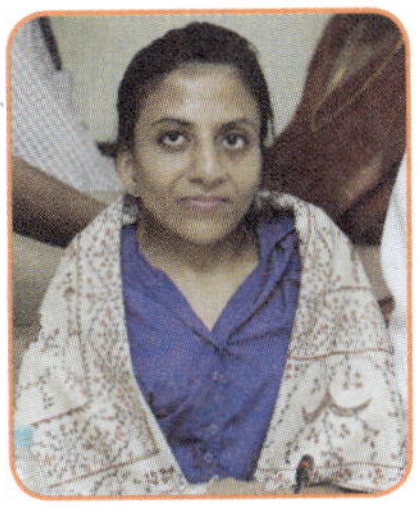

2. Ira Singhal

....

....

3. Ravindra Jain

....

....

4. Frida Kahlo

....

....

5. Sudha Chandran

....

....

6. Stephen Hawking

....

....

B. **Work in pairs and do a research on any two personalities mentioned in Exercise A. Find out about their disability and what they became famous for. Then, fill in the table based on your findings.**

Name of the personality	Kind of challenge faced	His/Her success story
1.	....	....
2.	....	....

C. **What are the different modes of transportation in your city? Discuss the facilities they provide for the differently abled.**

7 Fight, Manju, Fight!

–Sigrun Srivastav

OBJECTIVES

In this chapter, we will:

- *read the story about a girl with special needs.*
- *learn words related to disability, and spelling rules for words ending with -ing.*
- *learn about subject, predicate, and subject-verb agreement.*
- *listen and answer questions, and build a chain story.*
- *write a diary entry.*

4 QUALITY EDUCATION

10 REDUCED INEQUALITIES

READING

We often face various challenges in our day-to-day lives. When faced with such challenges, do you think encouragement from friends and family helps? Read a story about the challenges faced by a differently-abled girl who aspires to become a painter someday. Does she overcome the obstacles in her way?

Manjula Parelkar knew she was no Hussain. She could never be, not with those hands of hers, those claw-like malformed fingers, just two of them, two on each hand. Why her hands too? Wasn't it enough that her feet were deformed; ending in two massive moon-shaped toes pointing at each other, the hard nails touching, grating against each other whenever she wore wrong shoes. She wore wrong shoes most of the time, for there weren't any shoes in the market soft enough for her clumsy feet.

Her feet hurt most of the time, but she didn't mind them so much. She could hide them in those ugly made-to-order shoes. But she could not hide her hands, could she?

Manjula Parelkar knew she would never paint like Hussain, but she could learn to paint well. Handling brushes was no problem; they didn't feel any different from a pencil. Her problem was the cost of the materials she would need.

Hussain: a well-known modern painter
malformed: a part of the body that is deformed or misshapen
grating: (here) rubbing or scraping in an irritating and annoying way

'Mum,' she asked one evening while helping her mother in the kitchen after dinner, 'do you think I could...' she paused nervously, '... I could get some extra money tomorrow?'

'What do you need it for?' asked her mother gently, rinsing the dishes.

'For ice cream,' answered her brother from the door with an impish grin. Thumping the door with the palm of his hand, he chanted, 'We want ice cream! We want ice cream.' Ignoring him, her mother repeated, 'Why do you need the money, Manjula?'

'For colours and paints... I... I want to learn painting.'

'Painting?' asked her mother unbelievingly. 'Painting? But... you...' She added quickly, 'Of course, it's a nice hobby.'

'It will be more than a hobby,' replied Manjula quietly.

Mrs Parelkar looked at her daughter searchingly. She gazed long into those serious, melancholic eyes. Closing the tap, she walked over to the kitchen cupboard and pulled out an ornate, metal tea box from the topmost shelf.

'My piggy bank,' she smiled. 'Don't let out the hiding place.' Then she pressed a few notes into Manjula's hands. 'Go ahead and buy whatever you need, dear. Have fun and show me the painting.'

Manjula Parelkar showed her first painting to her mother the very next day.

'Manjula,' cried her mother dropping her needlework in surprise, 'why, that is beautiful! I didn't know you were this good.'

'Do you really think so?' asked Manjula doubtfully.

'Of course, dear,' she held the watercolour painting at arm's length. 'It looks perfect.'

'Oh, Mum!' cried Manjula pleased. 'This is just the beginning. I'll pick up fast.'

'I'm sure, you will,' her mother returned the painting.

'You must show it to Papa. He'll be impressed.'

Mr Parelkar pushed his glasses up and glanced at Manjula's work. 'Well done. Very good. A nice picture! See, what you can do!' Even though he didn't look at her hands with those claw-like malformed fingers, she knew what he meant. She swallowed dryly, something inside her twisting painfully. She knew the pain. She was used to it. 'Keep it up,' her father patted her settling in his favourite chair with the newspaper. He enquired, 'Is the tea ready?'

Arty Facts

- M. F. Hussain (1915–2011) was one of the most well-known modern painters. He also worked as a printmaker, photographer, and filmmaker.
- The Bombay Progressive Artists' Group was formed in 1947 by Hussain and his friends.

impish: mischievous; naughty in a playful way
searchingly: with a look intended to discover the truth about something
melancholic: very sad and unhappy
ornate: highly decorated with complicated patterns and shapes
needlework: sewing, stitching, or embroidery done by hand

'Why don't you frame it?' cried her brother Amol, snatching the sheet from Manjula's hands. 'Or, why don't you sell it?' Raising it over his head, he imitated an auctioneer, 'Two thousand rupees. Two thousand rupees. Who bids more? Two thousand one, two thousand two…'

'Amol,' his mother warned him. 'Put that painting down at once! Tell me, have you finished your homework?' The word 'homework' was enough to sober Amol. He crept to his room.

Manjula returned to her brushes and paints, and drifted into another world; a brighter world of glowing colours, beautiful forms and perfect shapes—the world where she wanted to belong so desperately.

Nobody had asked Manjula Parelkar what she wanted for her thirteenth birthday. But she got all she had secretly wished for.

'Oh Mother! Mother!' cried Manjula overwhelmed. 'A set of artist's watercolours. Thank you. Thank you so much!'

'And this is from your father.' Her mother pressed a book into her hands.

'*Painting—Step by Step*,' Manjula jumped in excitement, her dark eyes shining with happiness. 'Oh Papa, I could have never dreamt of this.'

'You wouldn't have dreamt of this present either,' said her brother with a mischievous smile, holding out a big parcel, tightly wrapped and knotted. Manjula eyed it suspiciously. Sometimes she wasn't too sure whether her brother was mischievous or simply mean.

But he wouldn't be mean on her birthday! She began undoing the tight knots and took off the wrapper only to find another knot staring at her. She hated unknotting parcels. Why did her brother do this to her?

'Bring her the scissors,' she heard her father's voice from behind.

'Why?' asked Amol annoyed. 'Isn't it fun?'

It wasn't fun. It was sheer torture. However, she struggled on with the knots, all eleven of them. When finally she managed to unravel the last one, she found a little box with a slip of paper inside. She knew what would be written on it: 'Sorry, better luck, next time!' It was just like Amol! Though he was only a year younger, sometimes she felt a hundred years older than him.

'Read it,' he urged.

She read, 'Look for the next clue under your pillow!'

'Oh no,' cried Manjula, but her brother pulled her to her bedroom. He even lifted the pillow for her. And there, tied with a pink ribbon, lay three watercolour brushes.

'Sable hair,' said her brother, 'artist's quality.'

auctioneer: a person whose work is selling things at an auction by calling out the prices offered by the bidders
sober: (here) restrain; make serious or calm
desperately: eagerly, very much
overwhelmed: overcome with happiness
mean: unkind
unravel: (here) untie
urged: constantly persuaded
sable: a small animal whose thick fur is used to make high-quality artists' brushes

She studied the new book from cover to cover and soon used up all her papers. She knew for good watercolour paintings, she needed special watercolour paper. But that was expensive.

'Mum,' she told her mother, pointing at the thin wobbly paper. 'I could do much better paintings on real watercolour paper. What do you think?'

'You are right,' replied her mother, 'but, oh… what a wonderful painting. You have improved a lot. I'll talk to Papa today.'

After dinner, when the children were in bed, Mrs Parelkar spoke to her husband about Manjula's paintings. Manjula did not understand why her father's voice was raised. He never raised it in front of her mother. With her heart thumping wildly, she tiptoed towards the drawing room and peeped in.

'Smita, please,' she heard her father say. 'Watercolour paper is expensive. And she won't need one only. She'll need dozens of them. Where will the money come from? It doesn't grow on trees.'

'I know,' her mother's voice was soft and pacifying. 'The price of petrol has gone up,' her father continued while pacing the room, 'the price of vegetables has shot up. Amol needs a new pair of shoes. These curtains need a change.' He stopped and looked at his wife tenderly, 'And you, you haven't had a new *sari* since last Diwali. Do you think I don't notice all this?'

Her mother turned her face away and whispered, 'I don't need a *sari*. I have enough to last me a lifetime. Let's buy her a few sheets to begin with.'

'Smita, Smita,' said Mr Parelkar wearily, 'it's not a matter of a few sheets. After watercolour, it will be oils, then canvases, and what not. Why does she want to paint, of all things? Why doesn't she learn something more useful, like cooking or stitching? With those hands of hers, she'll never become an artist.'

'Please,' cried her mother, 'don't say that ever again. Never. I tell you she has talent. Maybe we should show her paintings to an authority on art!'

Manjula Parelkar returned to her room. She didn't wait for an authority on art to see her paintings. She tore them up into bits—one by one, slowly, without shedding a tear, her claw-like fingers absolutely steady. She bundled up the watercolours and three brushes, all of best 'artist's quality' and tucked them away into the farthest corner of her cupboard.

'Mother,' she said the next day, coming into the kitchen, 'do you need some help in cooking?'

'Why, Manju, why?' her mother looked at her in surprise. 'Why, Manju, why?' she repeated, noticing the pain in her eyes.

'Because,' said Manjula, in as steady a voice as she could manage, 'because I think cooking is a useful thing.' Manjula Parelkar learned to cook, to fry, and to bake. She hated it. And she ate all she cooked, fried, and baked. She hated that the most.

'Heh! This curry is real good, Mum,' cried Amol. 'I'd like some more.'

'Manjula made it,' smiled Mrs Parelkar.

for good: finally, permanently
pacifying: causing someone who is angry to become calm
wearily: tiredly
canvas: a rough cloth used as a surface for oil painting

'Manjula?' asked her brother surprised. 'Cooking! Since when are you cooking? I thought you were into painting.'

'I stopped painting,' Manjula replied, keeping her eyes on her plate.

'But why?' Amol was shocked. 'You were so good at it. You must be crazy!'

'Amol,' his father scolded him, 'no such language in this house.'

'Sorry, Papa, but why must she do a dumb thing like this? I thought she would enter the *On-the-Spot Painting Competition* in November, at my school. Why, she would have easily bagged the first prize. Hey, Manju,' he turned to his sister, 'why don't you try for me?'

Silence hung over the dining table. Nobody spoke. Manjula waited, hoping for a word from her father. Her shoulders sagged when Mr Parelkar casually changed the topic. 'I have to go to Mumbai next week. There's an important meeting at the Taj. I'll need my suit. Could you take it out and get it ironed?'

'Mumbai,' thought Manjula Parelkar. She would like to go to Mumbai too. People were different there. They might not whisper about her hands when they see her for the first time. Or, give her that dreaded *Oh-God-poor-child* kind of look.' And there was an art college in Mumbai. Art! Manjula Parelkar was through with art. She had given it up for good. However much it hurt, however much.

'Manju,' her mother's voice reached her from far away, 'will you give me a hand?'

Manjula helped her mother take down the steel trunk. Mrs Parelkar opened it but then shut it again. She turned to Manju, decisively. 'Manju, I would like to talk to you. I....'

'Mother, please,' interrupted the girl, her dark eyes burning. 'Don't...'

'But, Manju...'

'Please, Mother! Please!'

Mrs Parelkar gripped her daughter firmly by the shoulders and looked her straight in the eyes. Her voice firm with determination, she said, 'Don't give in, Manju! There is so much in you that other girls don't have. Let it come up. Even if you have to fight. Fight, Manju, fight!'

Manjua felt a lump in her throat. She turned away from her mother.

'Manju, look at me,' her mother said gently. 'You have to learn to master obstacles. The will and the strength to overcome them can only come from within yourself.'

Manjula turned around in anguish. 'Stop preaching, Mother, just stop preaching. You see, it is... it is...'

'It is all Papa's fault,' she wanted to say, but deep inside she knew it wasn't.

crazy: foolish or mad
sagged: drooped, slumped or bent down
casually: in a relaxed way; not concerned about what is happening around
give in: quit, admit defeat
felt a lump in her throat: felt as though she might cry
obstacles: hurdles or problems
anguish: great mental suffering; extreme unhappiness
preaching: giving unwanted advice in a boring way

She dashed to her room, flung herself on the bed and buried her face in the pillow. But she couldn't cry. The tears just would not come. When at last she sat up, her eyes fell on a newspaper cutting on the table. 'Strange,' she thought, 'I didn't keep it there.' Puzzled, she picked it up and read, 'Playing football with artificial feet!' The bold heading screamed at her. 'In New Hampshire,' she read on, 'Rich Belanger who had lost his feet in a train accident, decided to play football with artificial feet. His coach thought it was ridiculous. His parents did not like it. (This sentence was underlined in red.) But Belanger stuck to it and made it to the Nashau team as the defensive end.'

Manjula Parelkar dropped the clipping. What a brave boy, she thought. He didn't give up. He played on, despite what other people said. Perhaps, her mother was right. She had to fight, fight on like Rich Belanger. Manjula walked over to her cupboard, hunted through the pile of clothes and pulled out her colours and brushes. She ran her thumb over the soft bristles, and the longing to paint, see and smell colours, drove tears into her eyes.

On the day of the *On-the-Spot Painting Competition*, shortly after breakfast, her brother said, 'I am off, Mum. Ratan and I are helping at the entrance gate. They are expecting a big crowd.' Turning to Manjula, he said casually, 'Pity, you aren't coming. I'm sure, you would have won a prize.'

'I might still win one,' Manjula replied as casually as she could. 'It'll depend on the subject in my category.'

'Your category?' cried Amol. 'Manju, heh! Does that mean you are participating?' He jumped up and pumped his hands up and down. 'I knew you would do it! I was sure you wouldn't give in.'

Manjula freed her hands and answered softly, 'If Rich Belanger could do it, why not Manjula Parelkar?'

Her brother looked at her, a broad smile spread over his face.

'Rich Belanger?' Mrs Parelkar asked, surprised. 'Who is Rich Belanger?'

'Rich Belanger,' spoke Manjula and her brother together, 'plays football with artificial feet. Isn't that something?'

Fact File

The Mouth and Foot Painting Artists Association (MFPA) is an internationally registered committee of artists. The artists use their mouth or feet to paint because of a disability caused at birth, or an accident or illness that prevents them from using their hands.

bristles: stiff hair attached on a brush

SUMMARY

The story is about a young girl who paints well but knows she could never become famous like M. F. Hussain due to her disability. On her thirteenth birthday, Manjula Parelkar receives everything she wishes for and takes up painting. Her mother and brother support her, but her father's growing pessimism and harsh words discourage Manjula to continue her passion for painting. Mrs Parelkar tries to talk some sense into her daughter by encouraging her to keep fighting. Her brother, Amol, is confident that if Manju participates in the upcoming drawing competition, she would certainly win. What really makes Manju change her mind was a newspaper article about a courageous young boy who plays football with artificial feet.

About the Author

Sigrun Srivastav (born 1943) is a Delhi-based author, sculptor, and illustrator of German origin. She has written and illustrated several children's books. She has also written scripts for television and children's films. One of her most popular books is *A Moment of Truth*. Her stories usually deal with the joys and fears of childhood, ecological problems, and the challenges faced by the poor and the differently abled.

COMPREHENSION

A. State whether these sentences are true (T) or false (F).

1. Manjula Parelkar knew she would never paint like Hussain. ☐
2. Manjula's father encouraged her to take up painting as a hobby. ☐
3. Mrs Parelkar gave her daughter a set of artist's watercolours on her birthday. ☐
4. There was an *On-the-Spot Painting Competition* at Amol's school. ☐
5. Rich Belanger played cricket with an artificial hand. ☐

B. Read the lines from the story and answer the questions.

1. *I didn't know you were this good.*
   a. Who said these words and to whom?
   b. What was the person good at?
   c. What was the speaker doing at that moment?
2. *Look for the next clue under your pillow.*
   a. What does this line refer to?
   b. What was kept under the pillow?
   c. Who had kept it there?
3. *'It is all Papa's fault,' she wanted to say, but deep inside she knew it wasn't.*
   a. Who wanted to say these lines and to whom?
   b. What was Papa's fault?
   c. Why does she eventually think that it was not Papa's fault?
4. *If Rich Belanger could do it, why not Manjula Parelkar?*
   a. Who said these words and to whom?
   b. Who was Rich Belanger? What did he do?
   c. What similarities did Manjula Parelkar have with Rich Belanger?

C. Think and answer the questions.

1. Why do you think Manjula knew she would never paint like Hussain? Was she right in thinking so?
2. What kind of a man was Manjula's father? Give evidence from the story to support your answer.
3. Why does Manjula's mother say, 'Fight, Manju, fight'? What does she want Manju to fight?
4. Who do you think left the newspaper clipping in Manjula's room with a sentence underlined in red? What does this tell us about the person?

Life Skills and Values

Empowering the differently abled

1. We often show sympathy towards people with disability. What, in your opinion, do they seek more—sympathy or equal opportunities to work in society? Give reasons for your answer.
2. When we see someone who is very different from us, we tend to feel uncomfortable. Why do you think that happens? Is it about them or about us? Is the difference only in physical appearance? What can we change in us so we are more accepting? Discuss.

VOCABULARY

A. Each word is a part of speech (noun, pronoun, adjective, verb, adverb, preposition, conjunction, or exclamation). It also has a meaning, an antonym, and a synonym. Complete the word webs for the given words. Look up a dictionary if required.

1.

Part of speech: ....

Meaning: ....
....
....

Antonym: .... — **deformed** — Synonym: ....

Sentence: ....
....

2.

Part of speech: ....

Meaning: ....
....
....

Antonym: .... — **dysfunction** — Synonym: ....

Sentence: ....
....

3.

Part of speech: ....

Meaning: ....
....
....

Antonym: ....

impairment

Synonym: ....

Sentence: ....
....
....

Spelling: doubling last letters

- There are certain spelling rules in British English when a word is changed from one form to another, especially when ending with *-ing*.
- If a word ends with a vowel followed by a consonant, and the stress is at the end of the word, then the last letter is doubled. For example:

  hop → hop + -ing → hopping

B. Change the words to *-ing* forms.

1. admit	4. clap	7. sip	10. stop ....
2. begin	5. get	8. sob	11. swim ....
3. chop	6. run	9. split	12. wed ....

GRAMMAR

Subject and Predicate

- A sentence can be divided into two parts—the subject and the predicate.
- The **subject** is the part of a sentence that names the person or thing the sentence is about.
- The **predicate** gives information about the subject. It usually contains the verb. For example:

  Manjula Parelkar showed her first painting to her mother the very next day.

  Subject: *Manjula Parelkar* — Verb: *showed* — Predicate: *showed her first painting to her mother the very next day*

Here, *Manjula Parelkar* is the subject of the sentence.

The rest of the sentence is the predicate because it tells us something about the subject.

Note that the predicate also contains the verb.

A. Read the sentences. Identify the subject and the predicate, and write them in the correct column.

1. Humpty Dumpty sat on a wall.
2. A rolling stone gathers no moss.
3. Each of these metals is found in India.
4. The consequence of crime is punishment.
5. A naughty boy threw a stone at the cat.
6. The colourful rainbow disappeared from the sky.

Subject	Predicate
1.	
2.	
3.	
4.	
5.	
6.	

Subject-verb agreement

- The subject and verb in a sentence must agree with one another in number. This means a singular subject takes a singular verb, whereas a plural subject takes a plural verb. For example:

  Watercolour paper is expensive.

  Here, the singular subject—*paper*—corresponds with the singular verb—*is*.
- Likewise, if the subject is plural, the verb must also be plural. For example:

  The paintings were beautiful.

  Here, the plural subject—*paintings*—corresponds with the plural verb—*were*.
- When two or more subjects are joined by *and*, we use the plural form of the verb. For example:

  The cows, the sheep, and the horses are grazing in the pasture.
- Two singular subjects connected by *either/or* or *neither/nor* take a singular verb. For example:

  Neither my father nor my mother is available at the moment.
- Note that the verb in an *either/or* or *neither/nor* sentence always agrees with the noun or pronoun nearest to it. For example:

  Either my cousins or my friend is going to help plan the surprise party for my grandma's sixtieth birthday.
- A singular verb is always used with distances, periods of time, or sums of money when considered as one unit. For example:

  Seven kilometers is too far to walk. *A thousand rupees is a high price.*

B. Fill in the blanks with a suitable verb that is in agreement with the subject.

1. Which answer is correct? Either .... (*is*/*are*) correct.
2. The cost of petrol .... (*has*/*have*) risen.
3. Either Ali or Rohan .... (*has*/*have*) broken the chair.
4. Fifty rupees .... (*is*/*are*) too much to pay for this pen.
5. *The Deathly Hallows* .... (*is*/*are*) written by J. K. Rowling.
6. Amol and Manjula .... (*is*/*are*) going to the painting exhibition.
7. A bouquet of bright flowers .... (*lend*/*lends*) colour to the room.
8. Either my aunt or my uncle .... (*is*/*are*) arriving by the eight o'clock ferry tomorrow.
9. Neither the king nor his ministers .... (*was*/*were*) present at the court musician's wedding.
10. Neither my classmates nor my friends .... (*is*/*are*) aware of the essay-writing competition.

LISTENING AND SPEAKING

Listening

A. Listen to the passage and answer the questions.

1. What kind of an environment has been created?
2. What will help the wheelchairs to reach the lifts easily?
3. What benefit will the visually impaired get once they are inside the lift?
4. What will help the differently abled to easily access the different sections of the station and the train?
5. Mention the three languages in which all announcements will be made.

Speaking

B. Sit down in a circle to tell a chain story. Let the story be about a physically challenged person and his/her life achievements. The first person starts the story by saying the first sentence. The next person adds the second sentence. Continue to spin the yarn till everyone has said a sentence. The last sentence must give the story a sense of completion. Keep these points in mind.

- Name of the main character and the setting
- The kind of disability and its cause
- Challenges/hurdles faced by the person
- How did the person deal with those challenges?
- What happened in the end?

WRITING

Imagine you are Manjula Parelkar. Write a diary entry about the day you participated in the painting competition held at Amol's school. You can include these points in your entry.

- Date and venue of the event
- Age group of the participants and their category
- The actual experience—feelings, emotions, environment
- Results and your reaction

8 Arunima Sinha: On Top of the World

OBJECTIVES

In this chapter, we will:

- *read about the mountaineer, Arunima Sinha.*
- *learn about compound nouns, words related to mountaineering, and their origin.*
- *learn about transitive and intransitive verbs and types of sentences.*
- *talk about our greatest fear, and learn about word stress in compound nouns and compound words.*
- *write an interview.*

READING

Read this biographical account of India's first amputee mountaineer, who, despite her physical disabilities, conquered the highest peaks in the world.

'A disability remains a curse until one decides to change one's mindset.' This mantra inspired Arunima Sinha to grab a spot on top of the world.

A native of Ambedkar Nagar in Uttar Pradesh, Arunima belongs to a family that enjoys sports. Having lost her father at the age of three, Arunima faced regular travails such as unemployment and insecurities about her future, until one fateful night in 2011.

It was a train accident that changed her life forever. A national volleyball player, Arunima Sinha was travelling to Delhi from Lucknow, when she was thrown out of a running train by some miscreants who tried to steal her chain while she resisted. Falling out of the train, she hit an oncoming train and fell on to the tracks. Spending an entire night on the tracks, with rats gnawing at the gaping wounds in her leg, she called

amputee: someone who has had all or part of an arm or a leg cut off
travails: struggles that people face
miscreants: people who do something wrong or unlawful
gnawing: chewing or biting continuously

for help, but to no avail. Next morning, some villagers found her and took her to the local hospital, where doctors amputated her leg. Later, she was shifted to AIIMS, Delhi, and underwent multiple surgeries to get back on her feet.

An amputation, a prosthetic leg and painful wounds would have broken down many people; but Arunima was made of sterner stuff. With her family standing by her, she decided to grab life by the horns and conquer the most hazardous of mountains—the unforgiving Mount Everest. Mountaineering, in her state, would be the greatest challenge to overcome.

Arunima Sinha removing her prosthetic leg near an indoor climbing wall

The first step towards this goal was to meet Bachendri Pal, the first Indian woman to scale Everest. Arunima went to visit the mountaineer soon after she was discharged from hospital. Although Pal was encouraging, she warned Sinha that it would be a formidable task to achieve the trek. She told her, 'Arunima, in this condition you made such a huge decision. Know that you have already conquered your inner Everest. Now you need to climb the mountain only to show the world what you are made of.'

Spurred on by the encouragement from friends and family, Arunima prepared for the longest journey of her life, and possibly the most arduous.

The trek to the summit has always been the ultimate test of endurance, even for the fittest of people. Arunima's trek, was, in many ways, her litmus test. The amputee started her training even before she was completely healed and worked relentlessly for two long years before making it to Everest Base Camp. She sustained various injuries during

amputated: cut off a limb by surgical operation
prosthetic: an artificial device that is used to replace a missing limb
hazardous: dangerous
formidable: something that inspires fear or respect because it is intense or powerful
arduous: something that requires a lot of effort because it is difficult

the journey. She would need to repeatedly adjust her prosthetic leg, which made it difficult for the mountaineer to continue the trek at the same pace as before.

Arunima's challenges didn't end here. Mountaineering is an expensive undertaking. Some say the only thing tougher than climbing a mountain is raising the fund for it. Most ardent mountaineers seek sponsors to fund their climbs, simply because they cannot afford them. Arunima faced many rejections while looking for sponsors. Not many companies she approached were willing to pledge their money on an amputee whose wounds had not healed. Meeting the requirement for her trek—close to 60 lakh rupees was nothing less than an ordeal. Nonetheless, her trek to the Base Camp changed perceptions, and she started receiving sponsorships. Tata Steel Adventure Foundation became one of her main sponsors. She enrolled in the Nehru Institute of Mountaineering and trained in the mountains of Ladakh, Uttarakhand, and Nepal before she tackled Everest.

Fact File

- While the oxygen saturation in a human body is normally 98–99 per cent, it reaches as low as 40 per cent at the summit of Everest.

Her Sherpa, Neema Kancha, and she trekked to the summit despite various odds. At many points during the ascent, she was faced with hurdles that would have daunted anyone. There were crevasses so wide that she had to jump without the help of a rope or a ladder—some yawning gaps that would lead to death if she missed so much as a step! She also had to listen to people goading her about her slow pace, while others admired her fortitude. However, Arunima persevered through it all, even crawling at some points during the journey.

Sinha recounts the breathtaking scene of ice-tipped peaks piercing the inky sky and how it struck terror in her heart with its sheer magnitude.

On the morning of the trek from the final camp to the summit, her Sherpa and Arunima were the first to start. The sight of dead bodies strewn across their path was appalling, but she did not let that deter her. In spite of being the first to leave the camp, their progress was so slow that many climbers overtook them during the day. Nevertheless, they trudged on, until the Sherpa conveyed the disheartening news that Arunima's oxygen supply was critically low, and she would have to turn back immediately. Having come so close to achieving her dream, Arunima refused to abandon the trek. Nothing would stop her now, even the morbid possibility of facing death if she ran out of oxygen!

Two hours later, they were at the peak! The Sherpa, who was unwilling to climb without oxygen and wanted to try the next day, spurred on by the woman who would not take no for an answer. Upon reaching the summit, Arunima unfurled the Indian flag and used the last reserves of oxygen to click pictures and take videos of herself to commemorate the greatest achievement of her life, until then. 'As I reached the peak, I wanted to scream to all my detractors, who thought a woman, an amputee, a middle-class person could never achieve the extraordinary. Yet, there I was, on top of the world,' said the achiever.

ardent: passionate about one's work
ordeal: a problem that exists for a long time
perceptions: the impressions you have of something or someone
Sherpa: a skilled mountain climber living in the Himalayas who is often employed to help visiting climbers
daunted: prevented or discouraged from acting because of fear
crevasses: large, deep cracks in thick ice or rock
yawning: (here) large and wide, and frightening
fortitude: to show courage when faced with a problem
morbid: extremely unpleasant; usually associated with death
detractors: people who discourage someone from doing something

Earth Speak

- The Seven Summits are the highest mountains of each of the seven continents. They are Everest (Asia), Aconcagua (South America), Denali (North America), Kilimanjaro (Africa), Elbrus (Europe), Vinson Massif (Antarctica) and Kosciuszko (Australia).
- The glaciers on Everest are melting rapidly due to global warming, giving rise to new crevasses that can prove deadly to mountaineers who are caught unawares.

The descent, as many would attest, is the toughest part of the trek to Everest. Tired beyond measure, one's body begins to give up and most mistakes are made during the trip back to the camps. Avalanches, snow drifts, and hidden crevasses only add to the dangers. Many an experienced climber has walked into death traps, but Arunima's good fortune did not run out on her. Fifty steps into the descent, her oxygen ran out, and she lay gasping for breath. Luck favoured her brave heart, as a British climber discarded his extra oxygen cylinder on his way back from the summit. Arunima's Sherpa helped her fix it to her mask to ensure that she had enough oxygen on her descent.

After making her country proud, Arunima went on to scale the highest peaks of each continent, called the Seven Summits. Her feats brought her many accolades, the Padma Shri and the Tenzing Norgay National Adventure Award, to name a few.

President Pranab Mukherjee honouring mountaineer Arunima Sinha with Tenzing Norgay Adventure Award at a ceremony at Rashtrapati Bhavan in New Delhi, August 2015

Today, Arunima Sinha is a name that brings joy and pride to every Indian. She has proven time and again that a disability is no reason to put a hold on your dreams. A motivational speaker, she has inspired many people to break free from the shackles of both body and mind and pursue their dreams. She has also set up an eponymous foundation for the empowerment of disabled women and children, and plans to set up a sports academy for the underprivileged and physically challenged. When counting her blessings, the accident that caused her to lose a leg and become an amputee figures at the top of her list. In the words of the world's first female amputee to conquer Everest, 'I would not have climbed Everest had I not met with the accident in 2011. Though I lost my leg, it made me a stronger person.'

shackles: physical or mental restrictions that stop a person from doing something he/she wants

SUMMARY

Arunima Sinha lost her leg in a train accident but found a new ambition to keep herself going. She aimed to scale Mount Everest, started training for it, and approached Bachendri Pal to be her mentor. After numerous challenges and conflicts, she managed to find sponsors and successfully reached the summit. Even when she was about to reach the peak, she was faced with the problem of depleting oxygen supplies; but luck favoured her brave soul. Arunima Sinha finally proved that with strength and fortitude, no summit is too high to scale. She is the first Indian woman amputee to conquer Everest, and has since scaled the highest peaks of the seven continents of the world.

COMPREHENSION

A. Complete the sentences.

1. Arunima Sinha is a native of ....
2. She was a national level .... player before her accident.
3. Arunima lost a .... in the accident.
4. The first Indian woman to scale Everest was ....
5. Arunima trained for almost .... years before she made it to Everest Base Camp.
6. .... became one of her primary sponsors.
7. The institute that Arunima enrolled in to train for Everest was ....
8. The toughest part of the trek to Everest is the ....

B. Answer the questions briefly.

1. Why did Arunima approach Bachendri Pal?
2. Why did the Sherpa ask Arunima to return before reaching the peak?
3. Why do mountaineers seek sponsors?

4. What are some of the dangers that mountaineers must face on Everest?
5. What does Arunima do to inspire more people to reach their goals?

C. Think and answer the questions.

1. How did Sinha prove that a physical disability cannot prevent someone from achieving their dreams?
2. What kind of childhood must Arunima have had? Give reasons for your answer.

Life Skills and Values

Determination and outlook

1. Talk about the necessary qualities one must have to achieve big goals in life.
2. How does a positive outlook help? Share your thoughts.

VOCABULARY

Compound nouns

- A **compound noun** is made up of two or more different words.
- It usually follows any of these structures to create a new word.
  noun + noun (*volleyball, website*)
  adjective + noun (*nobleman, small talk*)
  verb + noun (*go-kart, runway*)
- Compound words contain a headword or noun and a modifier. For example:
  snow (modifier) + flake (headword) = snowflake
  living (modifier) + room (headword) = living room
- Some compound nouns are written with space between the headword and the modifier, as in the case of *living room*, while some are written as one word, as in *snowflake*. It can also be hyphenated, as in *go-kart*.

Find these words related to mountaineering in the word grid.

1. summit	5. peak	9. oxygen	13. scale
2. ice	6. avalanche	10. crevasse	14. anchor
3. boulder	7. glacier	11. rope	15. headwall
4. scramble	8. Sherpa	12. climb	16. rescue

S	U	M	M	I	T	W	O	C	E	R	B
C	L	I	M	B	F	E	X	R	I	T	O
A	N	C	H	O	R	A	Y	E	N	G	U
R	E	S	T	M	E	K	G	V	I	A	L
E	T	P	E	A	K	G	E	A	N	E	D
R	O	P	E	S	T	L	N	S	A	G	E
Y	G	R	I	M	E	A	R	S	O	N	R
A	V	A	L	A	N	C	H	E	S	S	T
S	P	U	R	T	H	I	N	G	S	C	T
A	W	E	S	S	H	E	R	P	A	A	M
E	A	G	L	S	C	R	A	M	B	L	E
H	E	A	D	W	A	L	L	E	G	E	I
A	M	B	U	L	A	N	C	E	T	O	C
P	I	C	K	A	X	R	E	S	C	U	E

DICTIONARY SKILLS

Find the origin of these words with the help of the Internet or dictionary.

1. avalanche
2. aider
3. cordelette
4. mountaineer
5. arque
6. cirque
7. belay
8. bergschrund
9. abseil
10. chockstone

GRAMMAR

Transitive and Intransitive Verbs

- **Transitive verbs** are used with an object. The object can be a noun or a noun phrase (article, adjective and noun). For example:

  Arunima faced the challenges.
  verb object

- Here are some common verbs that are usually used transitively:

ask	*buy*	*enjoy*	*find*	*get*	*like*
join	*lose*	*love*	*make*	*need*	*receive*
say	*suggest*	*take*	*use*	*want*	*watch*

- **Intransitive verbs** do not need an object. The intransitive verbs are followed either by a preposition or an adjective. Sometimes, the sentence ends with the intransitive verb. For example:

  Arunima was injured.
  verb

- Here are some common verbs that are usually used intransitively:

appear	*arrive*	*come*	*die*	*fall*	*happen*
lie	*live*	*rain*	*rise*	*wait*	*work*

A. Identify the verbs in these sentences and write if they are transitive (T) or intransitive (I).

1. My grandpa felt unwell. ☐
2. Meera giggled at the joke. ☐
3. The cheetah runs very fast. ☐
4. I like chocolate waffles with ice cream. ☐
5. Kabir hid the books from his naughty cousins. ☐
6. The injured boy sobbed quietly into his handkerchief. ☐
7. The intelligent girl recited an interesting but long poem. ☐
8. The coach selected many girls from my class for the basketball team. ☐
9. I sent you a message last evening. ☐
10. My best friend lives in Lucknow, the capital of Uttar Pradesh. ☐

B. Use these verbs to make sentences.

1. Transitive:	answer	drink	purchase	steal	telephone
2. Intransitive:	capsize	feel	laugh	sing	sleep

Types of Sentences

- There are four different types of sentences:
  - declarative sentence
  - interrogative sentence
  - imperative sentence
  - exclamative sentence

Declarative Sentence

- A **declarative sentence** makes a statement, provides a fact, or conveys information. Such sentences end with a full stop. For example:

  Arunima decided not to give up.
  The new session doesn't begin until April.

Interrogative Sentence

- An **interrogative sentence** is a question.
- This type of sentence always ends with a question mark. For example:

  What is a summit?
  Would you like to climb Everest?

Imperative Sentence

- An **imperative sentence** functions as a command or an instruction.
- This type of sentence can be used to offer advice, make a request or invite someone.
- An imperative sentence that is a type of command ends with a full stop or an exclamation mark. For example:

  Request: *Please pass the salt.*
  Command: *Hurry up! We are getting late.*
  Instruction: *Don't rush or you will fall.*

Exclamative Sentence

- An **exclamative sentence** usually expresses surprise or shock.
- This type of sentence always ends with an exclamation mark. For example:

  What an extraordinary mountaineer she is!
  What a wonderful painting!

C. Rearrange the words to make meaningful sentences, and add the correct punctuation marks. Identify the type of each sentence.

1. a do knife not play with ....
2. favourite is subject what your ....
3. beautiful house how that was ....
4. doing last Sunday you were what ....
5. by caught police the thief was the ....
6. by bus children the to travel school ....
7. medicines on please take time your ....
8. are boys football in the park playing the ....
9. hummingbird the tiniest bee bird is the ....
10. coral beautiful lakshwadeep reefs islands have ....
11. indian grow up i plan to the states visit all when i ....
12. books did during holidays how many read summer the you ....

D. Rewrite these sentences as directed.

1. This is his new car. (*convert to interrogative*)

   ....

2. What a naughty boy he is! (*convert to declarative*)

   ....

3. This is disappointing news. (*convert to exclamative*)

   ....

4. Could you pass me my glasses? (*convert to imperative*)

   ....

5. This is the most boring film I have watched. (*convert to exclamative*)

   ....

6. How kind your neighbour is! (*change to declarative*)

   ....

7. This a very touching poem. (*change to exclamative*)

   ....

8. Would you open the door, please? (*change to imperative*)

   ....

LISTENING AND SPEAKING

Listening

A. Listen to the passage. Then choose the correct option.

1. *Born Again on the Mountain* is written by
   a. Ira Singhal.
   b. Arunima Sinha.
   c. Bachendri Pal.
   d. Sudha Chandran.
2. The first major peak that Sinha scaled was
   a. Everest.
   b. Aconcagua.
   c. Denali.
   d. Elbrus.
3. It took Arunima over .... to reach Base Camp.
   a. an hour
   b. two hours
   c. one day
   d. two days
4. The area after Camp 3 is known as the ....
   a. Ice Zone
   b. Blue Zone
   c. Death Zone
   d. Base Camp

5. Arunima has a .... to prove her accomplishment.

a. flag
b. rock
c. rope
d. video

21st CENTURY SKILLS Communication

Speaking

B. Work in groups of five. Talk to your teammates about your greatest fear. Discuss these points.

- Why were you afraid?
- What advice was given to you, if any?
- What made you decide to face your fear?
- What steps did you take?
- Who helped you along the way?

Pronunciation

C. In compound nouns, the stress is on the first syllable or the first part of the compound noun. Read the words with stress on the first syllable.

1. flashlight
2. football
3. keyboard
4. sunlight
5. toothpaste
6. windmill

D. Compound verbs lay stress on the second syllable or the second component of the verb. Read the words with stress on the second syllable.

1. double click
2. outsmart
3. overtake
4. stir-fry
5. underestimate
6. waterproof

WRITING

Imagine you are studying journalism and got the rare opportunity to interview Arunima Sinha. Write a dialogue between you and Sinha, in the form of an interview. Cover these points.

- Her mental ability
- Her perseverance
- Motivational talks
- Why she chose to inspire people with her life
- Her opinion on global warming and its impact on mountaineering

Poem

9 I Speak Sign Language

–Sarah Ismail

OBJECTIVES

In this chapter, we will:

- *read the poem about people who use sign language.*
- *learn to use words related to communication.*
- *prepare a presentation, and recite the poem as a rhythmic rap song.*

10 REDUCED INEQUALITIES

READING

Communication is the means of sharing our feelings and thoughts with others. The most common mode of communication is verbal, or the use of spoken words. However, there are other forms of communication such as gestures and sign language too. Read this poem to find out more about those who use sign language.

I may not hear a single sound
My world may seem quiet for miles around
Your verbal speech is no use to me
But I have a language of my own, you see.

Subtitles are on when I watch the telly
I won't even blink at your rumbling belly!
You may look twice at what I call speech
But for me it keeps your world within reach.

I call it Sign Language, there are no other names
To those who can hear, it looks like fun 'n' games
But it's so much more for all its speakers
We have words for everything, from buses to beakers.

verbal: spoken; something that is expressed by using speech
subtitles: explanatory text that appear at the bottom of a video or a film
telly: television
rumbling: a continuous deep and low sound
beakers: glass or plastic jar-like containers without a handle used in chemistry laboratories for experiments

Communication, you see, doesn't have to be spoken
Sign Language fixed a volume switch that started out broken
We even have a dictionary
Filled with pictures though it may be.

My world may seem silent and lonely to you
But thanks to my language, that's not at all true
My language started small, but soon it grew
I speak Sign Language, can I teach it to you?

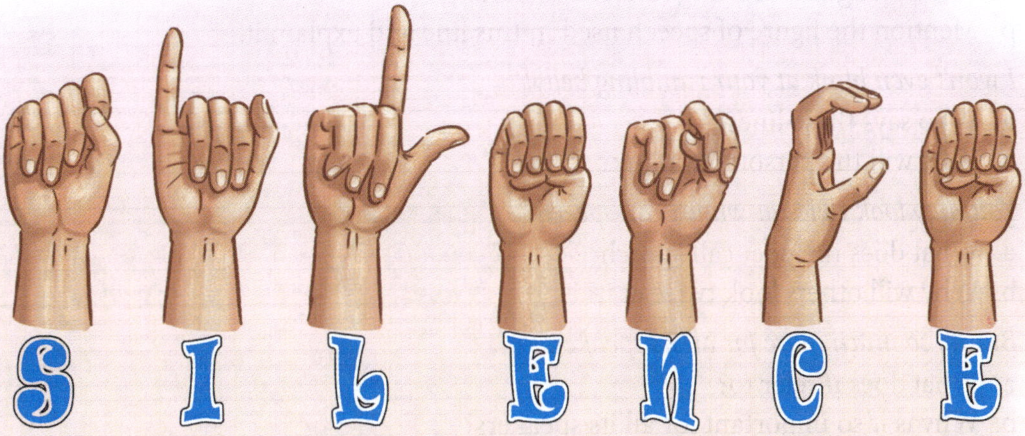

SUMMARY

Human beings share their feelings and thoughts with each other through the medium of communication. The most common mode of communication is the spoken word. However, the poet brings our attention to those who communicate with the help of sign language and gestures. She may not be able to hear a single sound, but it is sign language that helps her understand everything around her. She happily watches films and understands the plot through subtitles. She even boasts about using a dictionary filled with pictures. Sign language has enriched the poet's life in so many ways that she even wants to teach the language to others.

About the Poet

Sarah Ismail is a differently-abled writer, poet, and freelance journalist living in the United Kingdom. She writes about disabilities and issues related to them, taking inspiration from herself and her disabled friends. Her poetry collection *Listen to The Silence* is about life with a physical disability.

COMPREHENSION

A. Read the lines from the poem and answer the questions.

1. *My world may seem quiet for miles around*
   a. Who says these lines?
   b. Why is this person's world quiet?
2. *But for me it keeps your world within reach.*
   a. What does *it* refer to?
   b. Explain the phrase *keeps your world within reach.*
3. *My language started small, but soon it grew*
   a. Which language is being referred to here?
   b. Mention the figure of speech used in this line and explain it.
4. *I won't even blink at your rumbling belly!*
   a. Who says these lines?
   b. Why will the person not blink?
5. *You may look twice at what I call speech*
   a. What does the poet call speech?
   b. Why will others look twice at it?
6. *But it's so much more for all its speakers*
   a. What does *it* refer to?
   b. Why is *it* so important for all its speakers?

B. Answer the questions briefly.

1. Why is verbal speech of no use to the poet?
2. How does the poet enjoy watching television programmes?
3. According to the poet, what does sign language look like to others, and why?
4. How is the dictionary for sign language different from other dictionaries?

C. Think and answer the questions.

1. *Communication, you see, doesn't have to be spoken.* Explain this statement in the context of the poem.
2. *Sign Language fixed a volume switch that started out broken.* Explain.
3. What does the poet mean when she says that her *language started small, but soon it grew*?
4. In your opinion, what kind of an attitude does the poet have?
5. Why do you think the poet wants to teach everyone sign language? What do you think will be its effect?

Life Skills and Values

Self-respect

1. What are your strengths? What are the areas that you don't feel good about, in you? What are the ways that you can make these areas work for you to make it your strength? Discuss.
2. It is self-respect that determines your attitude and the way you feel about yourself. What does it mean to respect yourself? Give examples from your style of studying, playing, in your interactions with your classmates, family, seniors and juniors.

VOCABULARY

Fill in the blanks with suitable words related to communication.

discuss *gossip* *narrate* *recite* *shout* *speak* *talk* *whisper*

1. To .... is a bad habit.
2. Please do not .... as the baby is sleeping.
3. Ziad wanted to .... to his football coach.
4. Mary wanted to .... the poem that she had learnt.
5. The teacher asked her students to .... the incident.
6. Never be afraid to .... out against something that is wrong.
7. We decided to .... the matter before taking any decision.
8. Juhi's voice became a .... when Principal entered the class.

ACTIVITY

21st CENTURY SKILLS

ICT

A. Form groups of four. Look up the Internet to find out about the origin of sign language. Create a PowerPoint presentation based on your findings. Do cover these points.

- Who invented sign language
- Place and time of the origin of sign language
- Its advantages and disadvantages
- Modern day methods

B. The poem 'I Speak Sign Language' has a rhythm to it. Let's have some fun! Work in pairs and recite the poem like a rap song.

Unit 4: Toys and Games

WARM-UP

A. Write your five strengths or qualities on a sheet of paper. Then fold the sheet into a paper plane, and throw it across the classroom. The person on whom the paper plane lands, must pick it up, read out the facts, and guess who wrote them.

B. We usually play games with our friends. Sometimes, we have unusual playmates. Look at these children from around the world with their unique playmates. Which of these would you prefer to play with? Discuss.

C. Toys are an integral part of one's childhood. What kind of toys do you play with? Write their names here.

....

....

....

Now, tell your friends about the toys you have mentioned.

10 Powerful Moves

–T. V. Padma

OBJECTIVES

In this chapter, we will:

- *read the story of a wise man and a powerful king.*
- *learn and practise phrasal verbs.*
- *learn more about prepositions, and how to use the active and passive voice.*
- *give a motivational speech, and learn the pronunciation of words ending with -ed and different sounds of i.*
- *write a formal invitation.*

INDIA FOCUS

READING

We often feel that someone is powerful when they display physical strength. However, physical prowess is superficial and can diminish with age and time. The real strength of a person's character lies in his wisdom. Read this story to discover how wisdom overpowers physical strength.

There lived in ancient India a scholarly sage and innovative teacher called Sissa, the inventor of chess.

Everyone in the kingdom enjoyed playing chess, including Sheram, the king. One morning, as the king moved one of the gilded pieces on his marble chessboard, he asked, 'Who invented this remarkable game?'

'One of your own subjects, sire,' replied a courtier. 'A wise man by the name of Sissa.'

'I must reward this man. Request him to come to the court,' he commanded.

At once, a retinue of soldiers and courtiers sped off to Sissa's village, and the very next morning, he entered the king's court, dressed in well-worn clothes.

Looking Back

It is believed that chess originated in India and was originally known as *chaturanga*, literally the four divisions of military—infantry or foot soldiers, cavalry or soldiers on horses, charioteers, and elephants. Later it came to be known as *shatranj*.

scholarly: learned
innovative: creative
gilded: painted or covered with gold
sire: (archaic) sir
retinue: a group of attendants or servants

Looking at his simple demeanour, the king asked in surprise, 'You invented this game?'

Sissa smiled and nodded. The king looked at the sage and said, 'Ask for anything you desire and it shall be yours.'

Sissa thought hard. His silence troubled the king. 'Do not hesitate,' he said. 'You have to only tell me what you desire, and I shall give it to you.'

'Generous king,' said Sissa, 'I am a simple sage and my needs, too, are simple. I ask only for this: some grain from your granary.'

'Grain?' said the king in surprise. 'Surely! Do you want something else?'

'Grains of wheat are all that I want,' replied Sissa gently. 'As it is the power of my chessboard that brought me here, I ask that you give me grains of wheat in exchange for the squares on your chessboard. For the first square, I would like two grains of wheat. For the second, I would like two multiplied by itself, which is four grains of wheat. For the third, two must be multiplied by itself thrice, and for the fourth, two must be multiplied by itself four times. And so on, until the sixty-fourth square.'

'Is that all? Are you sure?'

'I am certain,' said Sissa. 'The grains of wheat you give me will follow the sequence 2, 4, 8, 16, and so on.'

'If this is what you wish, consider it given,' said the king. 'I took you for a wise man, but now I wonder! Take your sack of grain and you may return to your village.'

'I am an old man, sire,' said Sissa. 'Even a small sack of grain would be too heavy for me to carry. May I ask that you send this grain to my village?'

'Of course,' said the king. 'Your grain will reach you by sunset.'

Sissa smiled and left.

demeanour: appearance
granary: a building used for storing grain

The king spent the rest of the day busy with the affairs of his kingdom, leaving the prime minister to see to Sissa's reward. When the sun had almost set, the king realised that the prime minister had still not returned from the granary, and summoned him.

The prime minister walked up to the throne a few minutes later and stood nervously looking at the floor. 'Has that foolish sage's sack of grain been sent to him yet?' the king asked. The prime minister shook his head slowly, refusing to meet the king's eye.

'Why?' asked the king, exasperated.

'We are still counting the grains, Your Highness.'

'Still counting the grains?' thundered the king, getting angrier.

'What do you mean? If I don't send the sack, I will be breaking my word for the first time.'

The prime minister, raising his eyes at last, said, 'It is the sage's cleverness that may force you to reconsider your decision.'

The king shouted, 'I never reconsider! Get someone who is good at counting to help you, and make sure the reward is dispensed by sunset tomorrow.'

'I will do my best, sire,' said the prime minister.

The next evening, the king asked for the prime minister again. Instead, the royal astronomer, who was known for his skill with numbers and calculation, met him.

'Your Highness, I request your permission to speak.'

'What is that blundering fool doing?' yelled the king.

The astronomer calmly suggested, 'Why don't we sit down and talk it over?' He continued quickly, 'You do not have enough grain in your granary or enough money in your treasury to buy the amount of grain that you have promised to give him.'

'That's impossible!' hissed the king.

'Let me show you why,' said the astronomer.

With a flourish, he wrote down the numbers from 1 to 64 in a long column on the left of a scroll. 'For the first square on the chessboard, we owe Sissa just two grains of wheat. For the second, two is multiplied by itself, which is four grains of wheat. And so on, until the sixty-fourth square.'

'So what?' said the king.

'We must then add up all the wheat grains we get from the sequence of two from the first till the final square.'

'How long does that take?'

'Your Highness,' said the royal astronomer, 'I've no

affairs: matters
summoned: called
exasperated: irritated, annoyed
thundered: spoke loudly and angrily
dispensed: given
astronomer: an expert in the scientific study of the universe and its objects
blundering: careless
with a flourish: do something in a showy way so that people notice it
scroll: a roll of paper or similar material to write on

doubt that you will be able to work it out on your own. Why don't you tell us what the final figure is?'

'Sure!' said the king. 'I can do it in my head!'

He sat still for a few minutes, absorbed in calculation.

'Give me that scroll, would you please?' he said after a while. 'I am losing track of it in my head, with all those twos, but it will be easier on paper.'

The royal astronomer handed him the scroll and slipped away quietly. The king spent that night working out the problem. As the sun rose the next morning, the king summoned the prime minister.

The prime minister walked in, looking like a man who had not slept in a while.

'I spent the night working it out myself,' said the king. 'I know now why you were unable to fulfill my foolish promise. For the sixty-fourth square alone, we owe him about 18,446,744,073,709,600,000 grains! The royal architect told me that a cubic metre of wheat contains about 15,000,000 grains. I have been trying to imagine how large a granary could hold the amount of grain that Sissa requested.'

The prime minister nodded wearily. 'If all the land on Earth were sown with wheat, sire, it would still not yield the grain we have promised,' he said softly.

King Sheram smiled. 'Yes, yes, I know,' he said. 'You deserve some sleep, my good man. But before that, make sure you request that Sissa be brought to court again.'

The next day, when Sissa arrived, the king prostrated himself before the sage.

'You have humbled me,' he said. 'There is not enough grain in all the world to satisfy your request.' Sissa smiled.

'I don't need your grain,' he said. 'But there are many in your kingdom who do. Giving brings more joy and contentment than wealth and riches.'

The king bowed his head, and Sissa blessed him and departed.

Fact File

- A chess player of the highest level, who has won several international tournaments, is known as a Grandmaster.
- Viswanathan Anand became India's first Grandmaster in 1988.

yield: produce
prostrated: lay down flat on the ground, on your front, to show respect
humbled: (here) defeated and made someone realise that they are not as great as they thought they were
contentment: happiness and satisfaction

SUMMARY

The story revolves around Sissa, the scholarly sage and a powerful king. The king was fond of playing chess. When he discovered that the game was invented by Sissa, he commanded his courtiers to summon the old man to the court. Surprised by his simple demeanour, the king asked the sage to ask for anything his heart desired. After thinking hard, Sissa asked for grains of wheat in exchange for the squares on the chessboard. The king was taken aback by such a simple request and instructed his prime minister to send the sack of grains to Sissa. However, they later realised that the calculation is terribly complex, and that they would never have enough grains to fulfill Sissa's request. The king was finally humbled by the old scholar.

About the Author

Padma Venkatraman (born 1969), also known as **T. V. Padma**, is an Indian-born American author. She has written 20 books for young adults, including three novels: *A Time to Dance*, *Island's End*, and *Climbing the Stairs*.

COMPREHENSION

A. Choose the correct option.

1. The game of chess was invented by
   a. Sissa.
   b. Sheram, the king.
   c. the prime minister.
2. The king wanted the wise man to come to his court because he wanted to
   a. punish him.
   b. consult him.
   c. reward him.
3. What did Sissa want from the king?
   a. wheat grains
   b. a piece of land
   c. some gold coins

B. Answer these questions briefly.

1. Why was the king surprised on seeing Sissa?
2. The king had to give the sage grains based on a certain sequence. Explain the calculation.
3. Why did the king ask the royal astronomer for the scroll of paper?
4. What problem did the prime minister point out to the king regarding the reward?

C. Think and answer the questions.

1. Why did a simple request turn out to be such a difficult calculation? Discuss the magic of numbers in this context.
2. *Don't judge a book by its cover*. Explain this proverb with reference to the story.
3. The king was a powerful man while Sissa was a wise man. According to you, which quality is more important—power or wisdom? Why?

Life Skills and Values — Humility

1. What do you think was the intent of the sage in asking for grains with the mathematical puzzle? (Hint: Was it to humiliate the king?)
2. How do you display humility? Give instances from your day-to-day life.

VOCABULARY

A. Find two synonyms for these words.

1. inventor ....
2. reward ....
3. scroll ....
4. surprise ....
5. thundered ....
6. wise ....

Phrasal verbs

- A **phrasal verb** is formed by combining a verb with a preposition or an adverb.
- A phrasal verb does not mean the same as the verb itself. It changes according to the word that follows it. For example:

work out *make up for*

Here, the phrasal verb, *work out* could mean either *calculating* or *engaging in vigorous physical* exercise. This is different from the meaning of the verb, *work*.

Make up for means to compensate for something bad with something good. This is different from the meaning of the verb, *make*.

B. Look up the meaning of the phrasal verbs given in the box. Then, fill in the blanks with the appropriate form of the phrasal verbs.

play against *play along* *play around* *play at* *play back* *play off* *play up* *play with*

1. My younger brother loves to .... soft toys.
2. The children .... being wizards at the party.
3. Rafi often .... in class and disturbs everyone.
4. We were asked to .... the visiting team in the tournament.
5. The teacher asked the students to stop .... and get back to work.
6. I decided to .... with my friends in order to maintain peace in the class.
7. The two teams will .... on Monday to decide who will qualify for the finals.
8. The singer asked the musician to .... the portion recorded earlier.

GRAMMAR

Prepositions

- A **preposition** is used to show the relationship between two or more people, places, or things.
- A preposition is usually followed by a noun or a pronoun.
- There are over 100 prepositions used in the English language. Some of them are listed here.

by	*in*	*into*	*on*	*to*	*with*
above	*across*	*after*	*along*	*among*	*around*

before	*behind*	*below*	*beneath*	*beside*	*beyond*
past	*round*	*than*	*through*	*towards*	*underneath*

A. Fill in the blanks with a suitable preposition.

about *by* *down* *during* *into* *of* *opposite* *over* *since* *with*

1. Do not play .... fire.
2. The rat was chased .... a cat.
3. The horse jumped .... the fence.
4. My granny is fond .... chocolates.
5. I've not met my cousin .... 2019.
6. Meet me at the café .... the park.
7. My sister jumped .... the swimming pool.
8. I find it very difficult to sleep .... the flight.
9. His parents are happy .... his performance.
10. Would you like to walk .... the road to the milk booth with me?

Active and Passive Voice

- The **voice** of a sentence is the structure or word order within the sentence.

Active voice

- In the **active voice**, the subject or doer comes first, followed by a verb.
- A verb is said to be in the active voice when the subject does something or is the doer of the action. For example:

  I must reward this man. (Here, *I* is the subject.)
  His silence troubled the king. (Here, *His silence* is the subject.)

Passive voice

- In the **passive voice**, the action becomes the focus of the sentence rather than the doer.
- The subject or doer can be omitted, or it can be placed in a prepositional phrase, that is *by + subject.*
- A verb is said to be in the passive voice when something is done to the subject or the subject receives some action. For example:

  This man must be rewarded (by me).
  The king was troubled by his silence.

B. Identify the voice in these sentences. Then, change the voice and rewrite them.

1. I bought a new watch.
2. The police arrested the thief.
3. Mother was preparing dinner.
4. The farmer ploughed the field.
5. The watchman opened the door.
6. This book was published by Collins Learning.
7. The soldiers will be awarded for their bravery by the President.
8. Neha's parents gifted her a camera for her good performance in the exams.

LISTENING AND SPEAKING

Listening

A. Listen to a passage about India's first chess Grandmaster, Viswanathan Anand, and answer these questions.

Viswanathan Anand

1. When was Viswanathan Anand born?
2. Who introduced Anand to chess?
3. Where did Anand learn the intricacies of the game?
4. How old was Anand when he first started playing chess?
5. Which championship did Anand win by the time he was fourteen?
6. How many times did Anand win the National Premier Chess Championship tournament?
7. In which year did Anand win the International Grandmaster title?
8. Name the two famous chess champions whom Anand defeated in 1991.

Speaking

**B. Divide the class into six groups. Each group will prepare a motivational speech on acknowledging and accepting one's mistakes. Then each group will appoint a leader to present the speech in the class.
You may use these phrases.**

- I admit what I've done is wrong.
- I was the one to blame.
- I'm sorry. I shouldn't have done that.
- I never intended it that way.

Pronunciation

Verbs ending in *-ed*

- Certain verbs end with *-ed* when changed to the past tense.
- There are three different ways to pronounce words ending with *-ed*. For example:

Pronounced as *t*	Pronounced as *d*	Pronounced as *id*
laughed stopped	moved returned	attended dated

Different Sounds of *i*

- The letter *i* has three basic vowel sounds in English.
  - The long vowel sound. For example:

    kind *like* *line*

  - The second long sound. For example:

    machine *magazine*

  - The short vowel sound. For example:

    big *give* *list*

C. Say these words aloud, and find out if their endings are pronounced.

travelled studied started visited watched worked

D. Say these words aloud, and identify the three basic *i* sounds in them.

police sing six ski time write

WRITING

Imagine you are King Sheram. After realising the wisdom of Sage Sissa, you wish him to be part of your court periodically. Write a formal letter inviting the sage to the palace. You can use these phrases in your letter.

- cordially invited
- stay for a fortnight
- will be provided accommodation
- will be taken on a palace tour
- be a part of the proceedings in the court
- will engage in discussions with the king and other ministers

Free verse

11 The Tree House

–Sivakami Velliangiri

OBJECTIVES

In this chapter, we will:

- *read the poem about old, forgotten games.*
- *learn about imagery and write phrases.*
- *write steps to build a tree house and design a new toy.*

5 GENDER EQUALITY

INDIA FOCUS

READING

What are some of the games you usually play? Read this Indian poem about some children who build a tree house in a compound.

Come summer holidays, we built a tree house
in the back '*muttam*' of *Sarojini Amma's* compound.
In truth I had no idea about the geometry of it.
I merely helped with sawing of the planks
did all the odd jobs, but here every screw mattered.
After several afternoons of carpentry
all of a sudden *Chetan* fixed up the roof
the house was hoisted up, the ladder kicked away.
It could hold two children at a time. They
were all up on the branches. I was the last to go.
I looked down at the tool set that I had left behind
all open like reptile's teeth, baby-mouth-open-crocs.

compound: an enclosed area of land used for a particular purpose
muttam: a Malayalam word for *empty space around the house*
geometry: (here) the geometry of an object is the relationship of its parts to each other
Chetan: a Malayalam word for *elder brother*

It might have been a man's job, but when we are children,
boys can be girls and girls might be boys
unless a real bully came and bossed us around—
but then I had always a treasure chest of word weapons!

Literary Device

The poem is written in **free verse**, which means the poet does not follow any rhyme scheme. This style is used in modern poetry.

SUMMARY

The poem talks about how children enjoyed their summer holidays building a tree house in Sarojini Amma's compound. As the poet had no knowledge of measurements and construction, she could only help with sawing of the planks. After working for many afternoons, the children finished building a tree house that could hold two children at a time. The poet believes that doing such a thing might be a man's job alone, but no such rules apply to children. She also boasts about her rich vocabulary that she would use if a bully ever came around.

About the Poet

Sivakami Velliangiri was born in erstwhile Madras and raised in Trivandrum. Her poems are pleasantly Indian with many regional references. Professor Srinivasa Iyengar included her among the women poets in his *History of Indian Writing in English* (1980 edition).

COMPREHENSION

A. Read the lines from the poem and answer the questions.

1. *It could hold two children at a time.*
   a. What does 'it' refer to?
   b. Who fixed up its roof?
2. *...but then I had always a treasure chest of word weapons!*
   a. Who does 'I' refer to?
   b. What does 'I' mean by word weapons?

B. Answer these questions briefly.

1. When did the children build the tree house?
2. Where was it built?
3. How did the poet help?
4. Who was the last one to climb the tree?
5. What did the tool set look like?

C. Think and answer the questions.

1. What message is the poet trying to convey through the poem?
2. What do you think the poet means when she says—*but when we are children, boys can be girls and girls might be boys*?

Life Skills and Values

Games and gender

1. Children have played in nature for generations—be it playing in rainwater puddles, creating sandcastles, climbing trees, or chasing the moon and clouds. However, today technology seems to have taken over the pleasures of playing in nature. Do you agree with this statement? Express your views.
2. Do you think games should be played on the basis of gender? Why/Why not? Share your thoughts.

VOCABULARY

Imagery

- **Imagery** is a literary device used by writers to create pictures in the mind of the reader.
- Read this line.

All open like reptile's teeth, baby-mouth-open-crocs

Here, the poet evokes a sensory experience by describing the tool set kept on the ground as the open mouth of a baby crocodile.

A. Give any two examples of imagery from the poems you have read in this textbook.

B. We read phrases like *tree house* and *word weapons* in the poem. Now complete these phrases on your own.

1. magic ......wand......
2. travel ....
3. car ....
4. hot ....
5. musical ....
6. cold ....
7. washing ....
8. ticket ....
9. station ....
10. dining ....

ACTIVITY

A. In groups of five, write down the process involved in building a tree house. You can take the help of the Internet. Use the concept of a flow chart to ensure you follow the correct sequence. Follow the example.

First, we must look for a sturdy tree in our garden.

↓

Then we must decide on which branch we will build the tree house.

↓

B. Imagine Christmas is round the corner. Design a new toy for Santa's toy factory. Draw the toy and write three special features of the toy that makes it unique. HC

....

....

....

10 REDUCED INEQUALITIES

17 PARTNERSHIPS FOR THE GOALS

PROJECT 2

SPORTS & GAMES

The Paralympic Games are governed by International Paralympic Committee (IPC), which is the global governing body of the Paralympic Movement. These games were started with an aim to create a more inclusive society for people with a range of disabilities.

Para athletes are divided into different categories according to their level of physical impairment. They are given an opportunity to stand at par with others, excel in sports, and inspire the world with their relentless determination and strength.

Read and research more about Paralympic Games and answer the questions.

- When and where were the first Winter Paralympic Games held?
- What is the motto of the Paralympic movement?
- Name the host cities of the Paralympic Games.
- How many medals have Indian sportspersons won in Paralympics till now? Name three Indian medalists and their sport.
- Who is the first Indian woman to win a medal at the Paralympics?
- Which para athlete's story inspired you the most, and why?

Make a scrapbook and present your project creatively using pictures.

Unit 5: Health and Sanitation

WARM-UP

A. Our environment is continuously being harmed by various hazardous materials. Look at the pictures and discuss which of these are dangerous for the environment.

1. 

2. 

3. 

4. 

5. 

6. 

7. 

8. 

B. Discuss some alternative methods to prevent environmental degradation.

C. Look at these pictures of ragpickers and answer the questions.

1. In both the pictures, the children are earning for themselves. Do you think they are old enough to earn? Why do you think they choose to work?
2. Do these children face health risks? How?
3. Do you think ragpickers help protect the environment? Do you know what they do with the garbage they collect?

Short story

12 Children at Work

–Gita Wolf, Anushka Ravishanka

OBJECTIVES

In this chapter, we will:

- *read the story about a ragpicker.*
- *learn similes and make sentences.*
- *learn about adverbs and phrasal verbs.*
- *have a group discussion, and learn the difference between /s/ and /z/ sounds.*
- *write an autobiography.*

INDIA FOCUS

1 NO POVERTY

2 ZERO HUNGER

READING

Have you ever seen poor children carrying huge bags over their shoulders, picking up rubbish like discarded water bottles, and plastic bags? Read this story about a child who left his home, looking for a livelihood.

When the Kanyakumari Express pulled in at Chennai Central, it took Velu some time to get off. When he finally stood on the platform, his legs felt wobbly, as if he was still on a moving train.

Velu sat on a bench on the platform, putting his small bundle down. Exhausted, he rested his head on his knees. He had eaten nothing but some peanuts and a piece of jaggery since he had run away two days ago.

wobbly: shaky, unsteady
jaggery: a type of solid dark sugar made from sugarcane or from the liquid found inside the fruit of certain palm trees

'*Aiy*! What, new to town, eh?' called out a rough voice.

Velu opened his eyes and turned around. Behind him was a girl around his own age. She carried a huge sack on one shoulder. Her hair was stiff and brownish, and she was picking up dirty plastic cups from the floor and stuffing them into her sack.

'No need to stare. What's your name?'

'Velu,' muttered Velu, looking away.

'So, Mr Velu,' said the girl, looking at his bundle. 'Ran away from home?'

Velu didn't answer. He didn't want to tell some strange girl what he had done. He had run away because he couldn't stand his uncle beating him for one more day.

'Don't think I don't know. This place is full of children like you. So, what are you going to do here? Become rich?'

She sat down next to him. Velu shifted away slightly.

'Hungry?' asked the girl. 'You won't get food by sitting here. I can find some if you want.'

She picked up her sack and started to walk away. Velu wondered what he should do. She was disappearing into the crowd, so he had to make up his mind quickly. He jumped up and ran after her.

He caught up with her as she was leaving the station. The vehicles kept coming and never stopped for anyone. Velu kept hesitating and the girl finally dragged him to the other side.

'What do you think you're doing?'

They walked along the side of the road and turned onto a wide bridge and walked up. Velu looked around. In the distance, he could see huge buildings and towers and more roads.

'See that big building with the wall around it? If you're not careful, you'll soon be counting bars there,' the girl grinned.

Velu read the Tamil sign: *Central Jail*. 'Why? I haven't done anything wrong.'

'You don't have to do anything. Just don't get caught,' said the girl, heading down the bridge with the sack on her shoulder.

'What are you carrying in that bag?'

'Things. Bottles, paper.'

Velu felt too shy to ask what she was doing with them.

The sun blasted down on the tar and Velu's bare feet burned. After almost an hour, they stopped in front of a big building. 'Sri Raja Rajeshwari Prasanna Kalyana Mandapam,' read Velu slowly.

'Come on,' she said.

'Are we going to eat here?' asked Velu, looking at the huge hall and the people inside.

aiy: an exclamation used to attract someone's attention
stare: to look at somebody for a long time
hesitating: being unwilling to do something because you are unsure it is the right thing to do
grinned: smiled broadly
blasted down: (here) burned down; shone brightly
tar: a thick black sticky substance used especially for making roads

'Such high hopes!' said the girl, shaking her thumb under his nose.

She led him behind the hall. There was a big garbage bin overflowing with rubbish. There was a rotten smell in the air. The girl picked up a squashy banana and held it out to Velu.

'Here's your food.'

Velu was shocked. 'Are we going to eat their leftovers?'

'*Chey*! I only take untouched food. Here, some more... catch!' She threw him a *vada*. Velu looked at it with distaste.

'Come on, eat it! You think I like it? I told you I'll find you something to eat. You'd better eat what you get until you have your own money.'

Velu hesitated, but his stomach twisted with hunger. He gulped down the banana and *vada*. He could have eaten at least ten times more, but the girl could find only one more banana which she ate herself.

'It's too early, they've only eaten tiffin. If you're still hungry, you'll have to wait for them to finish lunch. I have to work; I'm going.' She picked up a couple of bottles from the heap and threw them into her sack and walked off.

Velu panicked. If the girl left him, he had no idea where he was and what to do.

He ran after her again.

'*Aiy*, what is your name?' he asked, hurrying behind her.

She stopped and turned around. 'So you've been following me around without even knowing my name. Jaya.'

'Can I come with you?'

'Come if you want. This bag is full; I have to go home to get another one.'

Jaya and Velu walked along the roads for half an hour, until they came to a bridge across a dirty trickle of water. 'We are in Triplicane now. That's Buckingham Canal,' said Jaya.

That was a canal?

Near some puddles was a row of the strangest huts he had ever seen. They were built out of metal sheets, tyres, bricks, wood, and plastic. They stood crookedly and looked as if they would fall any moment.

Jaya went around to one of the huts and dumped her sack outside and picked up an empty one.

'Let's go.'

She turned to Velu and gave him a push. 'Here, wear these and come with me.'

She threw him a pair of old shoes without laces and pushed a sack and a stick into his hands. Velu was confused. What work did she want him to do with these things? The only work he had ever done was on the landowner's farm at home.

squashy: very ripe and soft
leftovers: uneaten food that remains after a meal
chey: an expression of strong disgust
vada: a savoury dish made by deep-frying a ball of ground pulses
distaste: a dislike for something unpleasant
tiffin: a light meal or snack, especially one taken at midday
panicked: had a very strong feeling of anxiety or fear
crookedly: bent or twisted

'Are there any farms here?' he asked Jaya.

She laughed and thumped her stick on the ground. 'There are no farms here! We are ragpickers. See my sack? Full of things I collected.'

'Collected? From where?' asked Velu.

'From rubbish bins, where else?'

'You collect rubbish?' Velu had never heard of such a thing.

'Yes, blockhead. It's not any rubbish. Only paper, plastic, glass, such things. We sell it to Jam Bazaar Jaggu.'

Velu had heard of people throwing away rubbish. But why would anyone want to buy rubbish?

'Who's Jam Bazaar Jaggu? Why's he buying all this?'

'He sells it to a factory. Come on, I don't have time to waste like you.'

Velu did not move. He hadn't come to this new place to dig through garbage bins.

Jaya poked at him with her stick.

'Look here!' she shouted. 'If someone gets there before us, we don't get anything. Don't just stand there. I'm trying to help you.'

blockhead: a foolish person
sighed: let out a deep breath (to express disappointment or tiredness)

Velu scratched his head and sighed. I'll do it for now, he thought, until I find a better job.

SUMMARY

Velu runs away from home and arrives at Chennai Central. At the station, he meets Jaya, a ragpicker. She instantly takes him under her wing by giving the hungry boy some leftover food from a dustbin. Soon after, the two children go to Jaya's house to pick up a new sack for collecting garbage. The innocent Velu thinks to take up the job until he finds a better one.

About the Author

This short story has been adapted from *Trash! Ragpicker Children and Recycling* written by **Gita Wolf, Anushka Ravishankar,** and **Orijit Sen**. Gita Wolf is a children's author and publisher. Anushka Ravishankar is also a popular children's author, well known for her funny stories, such as *Moin and the Monster*. Orijit Sen is a graphic designer who has also published graphic novels such as *River of Stories*.

COMPREHENSION

A. Complete the flowchart with the events in the story.

Velu arrived at Chennai Central. → He sat on a bench to rest. → A girl, ...

→ She offered to find him some food.

→ ....

→ She started walking away from Velu, and he hurried after her.

→ They walked out of the railway station, past big buildings till they reached ....

→ The girl gave him some food that she found in a dump near the wedding hall. Velu was ....

→ From there .... Velu decided to work with Jaya until he found a new job.

B. Answer these questions briefly.

1. How did Velu feel when he arrived at Chennai Central?
2. Who did Velu meet at the railway station?
3. Why did Velu decide to follow the girl?
4. Where did the girl take Velu at first?
5. Where did the girl finally take Velu?
6. Why do you think Jaya gave Velu a stick and a pair of shoes?
7. Who was Jam Bazaar Jaggu? What did he do?

C. Think and answer the questions.

1. Velu plans to be a ragpicker until he gets a better job. Do you think Velu will ever get a new job? Give reasons for your answer.
2. What do you think were Velu's fears when he arrived in the new city?
3. Jaya proudly says that she eats only untouched food, though it is from the dustbin. Share your thoughts on how her idea of hygiene and safety is different from yours.
4. Jaya, a little girl herself, decides to share her food and work with Velu. What does this tell you about her?

Life Skills and Values

Kindness

1. Jaya in the story had many admirable qualities—her resolve to move on with her life, work to earn, help Velu, to name a few. Discuss other qualities you find in her. Which one of her qualities touched you? Why?
2. There are many disturbing things this lesson mentions. Which are the ones that affected you? What would you like to do to help the situation?

VOCABULARY

Simile

- A **simile** is a figure of speech in which a comparison is made between two things which have some similarity.
- In a simile, we use the words *as* and *like* to make comparisons. For example:

  The girl fought alone, *as brave as a lion.*
  The boy runs *like a horse.*

A. Match the similes in Column A with their meanings in Column B.

Column A	Column B
1. as blind as a bat	a. freezing
2. as cold as ice	b. wonderful
3. as wise as an owl	c. to fly high
4. eat like a bird	d. full of wisdom
5. like a dream	e. to eat very little
6. to soar like an eagle	f. completely unable to see

B. Complete the sentences using suitable similes to describe Velu and Jaya.

as busy as a bee *as cool as a cucumber* *as innocent as a lamb* *as hungry as a bear*
like a frightened rabbit *like a hawk* *like a log* *like a moth to the flame*

Jaya and Velu walked along the road. Jaya appeared to be ...., as she went about her work, picking up trash from the rubbish heaps and sorting waste. Velu was drawn to her ...., knowing that she was the only kind soul in the strange city. Velu, ..., did not understand the dangers lying ahead of him, and how difficult life was going to be. His stomach growled, and he realised that he was ...., and would like something to eat. Jaya picked up some food from a garbage dump. She was .... when she handed it to Velu, who, unlike her, looked worried about eating something from the dustbin. When Jaya, who was watching Velu ...., asked him to eat what he had, he looked .... They walked and worked the whole day. At night, when they stopped to rest, Velu was exhausted and slept ....

C. Complete the sentences using the appropriate phrasal verbs in the correct tense.

call off *call out* *come across* *give up* *look after*

1. A nurse .... sick people.
2. I .... the article in the newspaper.
3. The match was .... because of rain.
4. The man .... to the vegetable vendor.
5. He .... because he thought he would fail.

D. Match the phrasal verbs with their meanings.

Phrasal verb	Meaning
1. catch up with something	a. chase
2. dig through	b. decide or plan
3. make up	c. leave a place
4. pick up something	d. linger
5. run after someone	e. reach someone who is ahead
6. stand around	f. search
7. walk off	g. take or gather

DICTIONARY SKILLS

Make meaningful sentences with these words. Look up a dictionary if required.

1. stiff 2. sludge 3. dumpster 4. landfill 5. compost

GRAMMAR

Adverbs

- **Adverbs** are used to describe verbs. For example:

  Velu shifted away slightly.
- Adverbs can be used
  - at the beginning of a sentence or a clause. For example:

    After almost an hour, they stopped in front of a big building.
  - in the middle of a sentence or a clause. For example:

    They stood crookedly and looked as if they would fall.
  - at the end of a sentence or a clause. For example:

    They looked as if they would fall any moment.

A. Place the adverbs correctly and rewrite the sentences in your notebook.

1. There goes it again.
2. Velu ate hungrily the food.
3. There was a small outside pond.
4. She steadily walked down the path.
5. The suddenly book fell off the table.
6. Quickly he had to make up his mind.
7. The train slowly pulled into the station.
8. The children loudly laughed at the clown.
9. They after the rain went to the restaurant.
10. Have you yet had lunch?

B. In your notebook, rewrite the sentences replacing the highlighted words with adverbs.

1. *In silence*, he followed the little girl.
2. Velu ate the food *with great hunger.*
3. He carried the bundle *without a care.*
4. Velu looked at the food *with distaste.*
5. The woman responded *in a rude manner.*
6. *The previous day*, they went to the circus.
7. The child knew where to find the keys *all the time.*
8. *In a slow manner*, the birds realised they were in danger.
9. *It is possible that* her train is late.
10. Do you meet your friends *many times*?

LISTENING AND SPEAKING

6 CLEAN WATER AND SANITATION

Listening

A. Listen carefully about a government campaign that aims to provide clean drinking water in schools. Match the parts to make meaningful sentences.

Column A	Column B
1. It is important that children	a. the health of school-going children.
2. In order to increase the attendance in schools,	b. attend school and get an education.
3. Another important factor is	c. where this program has been implemented.
4. WASH in schools aims to improve	d. a supply of clean drinking water must be ensured.
5. Children are healthier in schools	e. proper sanitation facilities and hygiene education.
6. They practice more hygienic measures at home and	f. pass on the message of good health being a consequence of good hygiene.
7. They become WASH ambassadors and	g. spread awareness about the same to family members.

Speaking

B. Work in pairs. Imagine one of you is a government health official and the other partner is a villager. Enact a role-play to highlight the importance of sanitation in your village. Cover these points in the role-play.

- problems faced in the village: lack of toilets, diseases and their spread, lack of funding
- solutions to these problems
- how should the government help

Pronunciation

/s/ and /z/ sound

- The letter *s* can be used to represent two sounds—/s/ and /z/.
- Words that begin with *s* usually use the /s/ sound. For example:

  screen *seed* *skip* *sunflower*
- Words ending with *t*, *p*, or *k* also use the /s/ sound. For example:

  sort *sap* *sack*
- Words that end with *s* can be either /s/ or /z/, depending on the sound before them. For example:

  bees *heads* *songs*
- Words ending with *d*, *g*, or *b* have the /z/ sound at the end.

  ends *eggs* *tubs*

C. Read these words aloud. Sort them into the correct column based on their pronunciation.

beds birds boys bugs cross crease friends
heads is noise serene ski smile song
striking summer sunny superb swift Thursday wise

/s/ sound	/z/ sound

WRITING

In the story, Velu is lost in Chennai and Jaya helps him and takes care of him. How do you think Jaya would have felt when she arrived in Chennai for the first time? Think of the circumstances that would have led her to become a ragpicker.

Imagine you are Jaya. Write a short autobiography.

You could write about:

- Where were you born?
- Why you moved to Chennai?
- How you became a ragpicker?
- What difficulties you would have faced?
- Do you want to be educated?
- What you want to become when you grow up?

13 What Can You Do?

OBJECTIVES

In this chapter, we will:

- *read the poem about one's environmental responsibility.*
- *learn about assonance, and identify the rhyme scheme.*
- *conduct a survey.*

12 RESPONSIBLE CONSUMPTION AND PRODUCTION

13 CLIMATE ACTION

READING

The Earth is in dire need of care. This poem tells us how little efforts taken by everyone will go a long way towards making our planet clean and green again.

When you see litter in the streets
And the air smells of pollution,
When you feel like it's all piling up
Remember there is a solution.

There's something each of us can do
To keep the rivers clean,
To keep fresh the air we breathe
And keep the forests green.

Help clean a beach
Or recycle bottles and cans,
Learn about the problems we face
And help others understand.

It doesn't have to be a lot
If we each just do our share,
So take time out on Earth Day
To show the Earth you care.

piling up: gathering in a pile, accumulating

SUMMARY

The poem brings our attention to the things each of us can do to make the Earth a happier and healthier place to live. We can get together to clean a beach, pick up litter, recycle plastic waste, and spread awareness about thoughtful environmental practices. The poet also mentions about Earth Day when the world comes together to celebrate the planet's natural resources.

COMPREHENSION

A. Read the lines from the poem and answer the questions.

1. *There's something each of us can do*
   a. What does the poet say that we can do?
   b. Why should each of us do something?
2. *Learn about the problems we face*
   a. What are the problems we face?
   b. How can we learn about them?
3. *So take time out on Earth Day*
   a. Why does the poet ask us to take time out on Earth Day?
   b. What does the phrase 'take time out' mean?

B. Answer these questions briefly.

1. What are the signs of pollution that the poet speaks of?
2. Do you think the poet is asking us to do a lot? Why?
3. How can we show the Earth that we care?

C. Think and answer the questions.

1. What is the message conveyed in the poem?
2. Do you think that caring for the Earth is like caring for ourselves? Why?

Life Skills and Values — Nurturing our planet

1. What are the five biggest problems the Earth is facing at present ? How do you think we can solve these problems?
2. There are many different ways in which humans are destroying forests. What are they? How can we nurture and keep our forests green?

VOCABULARY

Assonance

- **Assonance** is the repetition of vowel sounds in words that are close together. Usually, it is used in poetry to create rhythm or a musical effect. For example:

  When you see litter in the streets

  Here, the short vowel sound *i* is repeated in the line to create a musical effect.

A. Pick out examples of assonance from the poem. Indicate which sounds are repeated.

....

....

B. Underline and write down the vowel sound that has been repeated in each sentence.

1. Can Ann catch an ant?
2. Cut thin strips of tinfoil from the sheet.
3. An uneasy feeling was creeping over me.
4. The old men confessed that they were depressed and restless.

C. Identify the rhyme scheme used in the poem. Pick out lines from the poem to illustrate it.

....

....

ACTIVITY

Work in groups of four. Conduct a survey on the health and sanitation problems your city is battling with. The survey should cover these points:

- The major reasons behind environmental problems
- The most affected areas
- The places that are clean, and reasons behind their cleanliness
- The areas facing major health problems
- The government or citizen bodies or organisations that have been appointed to improve the situation

Unit 6: Ancient Wisdom

WARM-UP

The ancient and the modern world have had many great minds known for their wisdom. Match these famous philosophers and thinkers with their beliefs.

 1. Gautama Buddha	a. China's most famous philosopher believed empathy and education were the means to create a just society.
 2. Confucius	b. His name means 'the enlightened one', and he believed the root cause of suffering was ignorance.
 3. Socrates	c. This philosopher and freedom fighter believed that humans could evolve into divine beings through spiritual practice.
 4. Swami Vivekananda	d. Considered the father of Western philosophy, this great thinker believed in the importance of inquiry and analysis to get to the truth of things.
 5. Sri Aurobindo	e. The monk who introduced Hinduism to the Western World, believed that all humans are born good and education was key to keep that goodness intact.

14 The Story of the Anklet

OBJECTIVES

In this chapter, we will:

- *read the story about justice.*
- *find one-word substitutes for words.*
- *learn the modals can, could, may, might, will, shall, should, and must.*
- *learn about famous Indian epics, and enact a role-play.*
- *write a short story.*

READING

INDIA FOCUS

An epic is a long poem that tells a story of a great incident or act. Silappathikaram *is a poem about how no one, not even a king, is above the law, and any wrongdoer must face the consequences of their actions. Let us read on to see why the epic is named after an anklet.*

Kannagi and Kovalan decided to move to Madurai to start their lives anew, after Kovalan had depleted all their wealth. Since they had no possessions, a worried Kovalan lamented to his wife, 'How will we rekindle our fortunes now? The future is so uncertain.' Kannagi decided, 'We will sell one of the pair of anklets that I have.' This was the only ornament that still remained with her.

The couple began their journey during the last hours of the night, and on their way, they visited the sage Kavundi to seek her blessings. The saint decided to accompany them on their journey, and they walked for many days till they reached the banks of the Kaveri, and went further to reach the Vaigai—the river that flowed through Madurai.

At the outskirts of the city, Kovalan left his wife and Kavundi with some cowherds and told her, 'Stay here while I venture forth into Madurai so that I can seek our fortune here.'

anklet: an ornamental chain worn around the ankle
depleted: reduced an amount of something
rekindle: to cause something to happen again

Earth Speak

- The Vaigai is one of the major rivers of South India and is not perennial.
- It is an intermittent river that dries up during the summer.
- Since the river is the primary source of drinking water for many cities in Tamil Nadu, efforts are on to restore its water sources.

Fact File

- The legend of Kannagi has found resonance in Tamil Nadu and Kerala, where there are temples dedicated to her.
- Various sculptures and paintings depict scenes from *Silappathikaram* in these temples.
- Kannagi is known as Aatukal Devi in Kerala.

In many parts of India, people watch out for various omens before setting out for a new task. There were many ominous signs when Kovalan left the house. First, he left at an inauspicious time. Second, soon as he left, a humped bull stood in front of him and then passed him. But Kovalan, ignorant of these premonitions, walked towards the heart of the city, where the markets were, thinking, 'I will sell this ornament. With the money I make from it, I shall start a new business, and buy a simple house—so my loving wife, Kannagi, can live comfortably. We will be happy in this new city.'

On reaching the marketplace, Kovalan looked around him in awe, as he walked past shops that sold the finest cloth, ivory, furniture, and spices. He met a goldsmith and told him, 'I have come from afar. This is my wife's anklet. I would be honoured if you would take a look at it and tell me what it is worth.' Alas! Little did Kovalan know that he has met a crafty man. The goldsmith, a habitual liar and thief, looked at the ornament, and thought to himself, 'This looks like the queen's anklet which I stole recently. How lucky am I that this man has come to me to sell this jewel! Now, I can blame him for the theft, and escape the punishment.'

Chuckling to himself about his brilliant idea, the goldsmith told Kovalan, 'Please wait in my humble hut while I assess your precious anklet,' and hurried to the palace. The wily goldsmith, upon reaching the palace sought out the king, and said, 'O exalted one, the thief who stole from the palace is now staying in my lowly house, hiding himself from the watchmen of this city.' The king, who was eager to appease his angry wife, did not give much thought to the consequences of his actions. Having placed his trust in the goldsmith, he thundered to his guards,

omens: occurrences interpreted as signs of future happiness or disaster
ivory: a valuable substance which forms the tusks of elephants; also used for making precious ornaments
wily: someone who tricks people to achieve what they want
exalted: someone at a very high level in rank
appease: to stop someone from being angry by giving them what they want

execution: the carrying out of a death sentence
sovereign: (here) a king
retribution: punishment for a crime
trial: the hearing of statements in a law court in which a judge decides whether a person is guilty of a crime
inconsolable: very sad and cannot be comforted
proclaimed: made something known formally to the public
resentment: bitterness and anger that someone feels about something
audience: (here) a formal meeting with an important person
bewildered: very confused

'Set forth to the goldsmith's house. If you find the foot ornament of my queen in the possession of an expert thief, kill him, and bring the anklet to me.'

The guards marched to the goldsmith's house. Upon seeing Kovalan, one of the guards said, 'But he does not look like a thief! His appearance is not that of one deserving an execution.' However, the goldsmith laughed heartily, saying 'Pray, tell me how a thief looks... The king's guards are being fooled by a simple man! Look carefully, soldiers, this is the man who has stolen our queen's anklet. Should he go unpunished when our sovereign has ordered his execution?' Immediately, a soldier stepped forward and killed the innocent Kovalan.

Oblivious to her husband's fate, Kannagi was finishing her daily chores when a woman approached her, bearing terrible news, 'Your husband was executed by the palace guards. They were convinced that the anklet he tried to sell at the market was stolen from the queen, and so, the king ordered his death.' On hearing the news, Kannagi fainted.

Upon regaining consciousness, Kannagi clasped her husband's body, lamenting his death. She swore, 'I shall seek retribution for the injustice meted out to my husband.' Taking the remaining anklet as proof, Kannagi marched to the palace gates, wailing about her loss. She called out to the women of the city, 'Come with me, and help me get justice. Your king has murdered an innocent man. He has deprived me of my husband. He did not even give him a trial.' Hearing her wail, many people marched alongside her, and the crowd kept growing.

People sympathised with the inconsolable Kannagi, whose despair soon gave way to anger. Furious, she proclaimed, 'I shall avenge my husband's death. I will meet the cruel king and ask him to justify his actions.' So saying, she marched to the palace, followed by a crowd.

A guard at the king's court approached the king and said, 'A woman, filled with resentment and rage, awaits an audience with you. She waits at the gate, with an anklet in her hand.' The king, who suspected nothing amiss, was bewildered by this. He ordered that she be let in at once. On seeing Kannagi, who stood in court, eyes ablaze with fury, the king asked, 'What has brought you before us?' Kannagi replied,

'A man who had set out to sell a tinkling anklet was murdered by you, without a trial. I am his wife. I have come to seek justice.'

The king calmly informed her, 'It is not an injustice to put a thief to death; rather, it is kingly justice.' On hearing this, Kannagi declared in indignation, 'Oh, how you have fallen! Here, in my hand, I hold the

other anklet—the pair of the one that you falsely claim to have been stolen by my husband. Did you know that it contains gems within it?' So saying, she broke open the anklet that would prove her husband's innocence. Gems burst forth from the anklet, and the king watched with a mix of agony and horror—as they were not the gems in the queen's lost anklet.

Realising that he had committed an unforgivable crime, the king cried out, 'It is I who is the thief. The protection of my subjects has failed in my hands. Let me depart this life now,' and he fell down in a dead swoon, never to breathe again. Seeing her husband die, the virtuous queen also gave up her life, while the people watched, aghast. The death of these two noble souls was not, however, enough to appease Kannagi. She cursed the city of Madurai, saying, 'This is the city that has claimed my life, my love. A great fire will consume everything within its walls, except for the righteous saints and innocent women and children. Nothing shall remain of this, just as nothing remains in my life.'

The city burnt, for the gods justified Kannagi's wrath. But before all could be lost, Meenakshi, the goddess of the city of Madurai, descended upon Kannagi and told her, 'Your husband's death has been avenged now. Remember that you have also received your justice when the king and queen,

Looking Back

- *Silappathikaram* or 'The Tale of the Anklet' is the earliest Jain Tamil epic. It is set in two ancient kingdoms in the south – the Chola and the Pandya kingdoms.
- The Cholas and the Pandyas prided themselves on their integrity.
- Justice was of prime importance, and many rules were in place to ensure that punishments were meted out in accordance with the severity of the crime. It was believed that an unfair judgement reflected badly, not only on the king, but on the citizens of the kingdom as well.

indignation: the feeling of shock and anger when you experience something unjust
swoon: a faint, the state of becoming unconscious
righteous: morally good
wrath: extreme anger
descended: came down

relinquished: surrendered
apparition: an appearance of a ghostlike figure

who took the blame for the injustice, relinquished their lives for an act that was committed in haste. Is it not enough that so many lives have been lost?' After listening to the goddess, and seeing an apparition of her husband, Kannagi relented, and the destruction of the city ended.

- Adapted from Ilango Adigal's *Silappatikaram*

SUMMARY

Kannagi and Kovalan decide to start their life anew in Madurai. After they reach the city, Kovalan goes to the marketplace to sell one of Kannagi's anklets, which is their only possession. He approaches a goldsmith to sell the anklet. The goldsmith, who has stolen the queen's anklet, spots a striking resemblance between the two anklets and plans to blame Kovalan for the theft. The king believes the goldsmith and sends his guards to kill Kovalan. When Kannagi hears of her husband's death, she marches to the palace, demanding justice. She proves Kovalan's innocence by breaking open her anklet to show that it is different from the queen's. This grave injustice makes the king and queen surrender their lives, and Kannagi curses the city of Madurai to exact revenge.

About the Author

Ilango Adigal was a Jain monk, a Chera prince, and a poet. His most prominent work, *Silappathikaram*, is one of the Five Great Epics of Tamil literature. The poem describes a rich and cosmopolitan culture, where people from many different backgrounds such as the Greeks, Arabs and Tamils mingle, living and trading in the city of Madurai. Ilango Adigal believed that people from all sections of society could contribute to the arts, music and literature.

COMPREHENSION

A. Match the character traits of Kannagi with the different incidents in the story.

1. When Kovalan lost all the wealth	a. inconsolable
2. When moving to Madurai	b. vengeful
3. When she heard of Kovalan's death	c. optimistic
4. When she knew the reason behind Kovalan's death	d. furious
5. When she cursed the city	e. supportive

B. Answer these questions briefly.

1. Why did Kannagi and Kovalan decide to move to Madurai?
2. Whom did they meet on the way?
3. What did Kannagi give Kovalan and why?
4. Why did Kovalan go to the marketplace?

5. What happened when Kovalan met the goldsmith?
6. Why did the goldsmith ask Kovalan to wait in his house?
7. Why did the king order Kovalan's execution?
8. How did Kannagi react as soon as she heard of her husband's death?
9. Why did Kannagi march to the palace?
10. How did the king react when he learned about the great injustice?

C. Think and answer.

1. The king ordered Kovalan's execution without even giving him a trial. What do you think he could have done differently?
2. Justice should be served equally to everyone. Do you agree? Use examples from the story to support your views.

Life Skills and Values

Response and reaction

1. A decision taken impulsively because of intense emotion made Kovalan, Kannagi, the king and the queen react in an extreme manner. All led to even more sadness. How do you think it would have been different if each one had paused and given some thought to the way to proceed?
2. Think of any one incident where you have reacted on impulse instead of deliberating on a response. Tell about it to the class.

VOCABULARY

Replace the underlined words and phrases in the passage with suitable words from the box.

wailing *righteous* *ominous* *appease* *premonition*
habitual *oblivious to* *relinquished*

The king's court was shrouded in sorrow. The king had given up his throne and title because he wanted to pacify the council of ministers who were unhappy about a judgement he had made. Furthermore, the king's stepmother had had an inauspicious and threatening dream about the king being killed in court. There was a lot of crying as the king left the court. The virtuous king accepted that the punishment was fair and left the palace. When he was leaving, he had a foreboding that his kingdom was in grave danger, and entrusted his citizens' safety to his trusted advisor and prime minister. As is customary when a king is not in court, the council of ministers decided to choose a leader, unaware of the fact that the king had already chosen the leadership.

GRAMMAR

Modals

- **Modals** are a type of helping verbs.
- They are used to express ability, possibility, permission, or obligation.
- The verbs that are used as modals are *can*, *could*, *may*, *might*, *must*, *will*, *shall*, and *should*.

Can and *could*

- **Can** is used to show ability. For example:

    People can question an injustice.

- **Could** is also used to show ability. It is the past form of **can**. For example:

    Kannagi could not understand why her husband had been killed.

May and *might*

- **May** is used to indicate a possibility. For example:

    The couple may have stayed in Madurai.

- It is also used to denote permission. For example:

    The guard asked the king if he may send the protesters inside.

- **Might** is also used to indicate a possibility, but this possibility is less than that denoted with the use of *may*. For example:

    Kannagi might have spared the city of Madurai if she had known that the goldsmith was at fault.

Will and *shall*

- **Will** and **shall** are used to make predictions in the future. For example:

    The people know that the king will listen to Kannagi, and he shall grant her justice.

- **Shall** is more formal and much less common than **will**. It is usually used with *I* and *we*.

Should and *must*

- **Should** denotes a piece of advice or obligation. For example:

    Advice: *We should always listen to both sides of a story before passing any judgement.*

    Obligation: *Everyone should behave responsibly.*

- **Must** is used to denote a strong obligation or necessity. For example:

    Obligation: *The citizens must demand justice.*

    Necessity: *The king must pass judgement only after careful consideration.*

A. Choose the correct modals and fill in the blanks.

1. .... (*May/Might*) I come in?
2. It .... (*may/might*) rain today.

3. I .... (*can/could*) speak English fluently.
4. Sara .... (*can/could*) play the sitar when she was younger.
5. When .... (*shall/will*) we go for a coffee?
6. When .... (*shall/will*) you go for the musical?
7. The guests .... (*should/must*) be here any minute.
8. Passengers .... (*should/must*) fasten their seat belts.

B. Fill in the blanks with the appropriate modals.

1. They .... not understand why the king ordered the execution.
2. The man predicted that it .... rain.
3. Kannagi knew that they .... have a bright future in Madurai.
4. Kings and queens .... administer justice.
5. The guards .... not allow people to enter the court without permission.

C. In addition to their function of showing obligation, possibility, or permission, the modals *could, might*, and *would* are also used as the past tense of *can, may*, and *will* respectively. Rewrite these sentences by replacing the modals with their past tense forms.

1. They may leave after the concert.
2. Will he like to be interviewed about his work?
3. She may have visited her grandparents last week.
4. We can meet the prime minister at the conference.
5. They will be happy to meet the delegates from Australia.

LISTENING AND SPEAKING

Listening

A. Listen to the descriptions of some Indian epics. Match each epic with its famous historical incident.

1. *The Mahabharata*	a. The Battle of Troy
2. *The Ramayana*	b. The Fall of Man
3. *The Iliad*	c. The Battle of Kurukshetra
4. *Paradise Lost*	d. The Burning of Madurai
5. *Silappathikaram*	e. The Battle of Lanka

Speaking

B. Work in pairs. Imagine one of you is the king of Madurai and the other is the goldsmith. How would you have handled the case of the anklet theft? Talk about these points.

- the evidence that is presented
- the argument to establish the thief
- the punishment

WRITING

Short story

- A **short story** is a prose narrative which is shorter than a novel, especially one that focuses on a single theme.
- A short story usually consists of these elements:
  - an introductory paragraph that introduces the characters and the plot
  - details about the characters and the plot
  - a setting and context
  - a problem
  - a solution to the problem
  - a conclusion or ending

Write a short story about justice. Make sure your narrative covers each of the elements mentioned above.

15 Eat From the Edges

–Supriya Karunakaran

OBJECTIVES

In this chapter, we will:

- *read the play about Chanakya's wisdom.*
- *identify common proverbs, learn to use same words as different parts of speech, and use the suffixes -ible and -able.*
- *learn the use of future tense, direct speech, indirect speech, and reporting verbs.*
- *do a role-play.*
- *write a letter narrating an experience.*

INDIA FOCUS

READING

Two important people, a future king and his teacher, are discussing war strategies after another defeat. They take rest in an old woman's hut. They hear her giving a piece of advice to her grandson and decide to use it. Read on to find out what that piece of advice was.

Characters

- ***Chanakya:*** a 40-year-old ascetic, dressed in saffron robes with his long hair left unbound because of a vow of vengeance
- ***Chandragupta:*** a tall, well-built young man wearing an armour, helmet, and carrying a sword
- ***An old woman:*** a 70-year-old woman wearing a shabby, white sari and blouse, patched roughly in several places
- ***Hari:*** a young boy of about 10, wearing a patched *dhoti*

ascetic: a monk who leads a simple and strict life
vengeance: revenge
armour: a special metal clothing worn by soldiers in former times
dhoti: a long piece of cloth, tied round the waist, usually worn by men in India

[Chanakya and Chandragupta enter the stage from left and approach an old thatched hut, that is badly in need of repair.]

Chandragupta: Mother, Mother?
[The old woman comes out of the hut.]

Old woman: Yes, my son? What do you want?

Chandragupta: Water, Mother. Water. We are thirsty.

[The old woman takes two small mud pots and dips them into a larger mud pot and gives some water to him and Chanakya. They drink thirstily and drink again and again, for both are battle-stained and weary.]

Chandragupta: Thank you, Mother.

Chanakya: Thank you, Mother.

Chandragupta: Can we sit here for a while and rest, Mother? We have been in a battle, and we are exhausted and need to rest for a bit before we move on.

Old woman: Yes, my son. My hut is old and leaking, but it is yours. Please rest here for as long as you want to. Was it a great battle my son? Did you win?

Chandragupta: It was a great battle, Mother, and we fought till we bled, but we lost. Again!

Old woman: Rest now my son.

weary: very tired
exhausted: physically and mentally tired
for a bit: for a short time

[She enters her hut. Her grandson is playing outside at the right side of the stage with a string and top. Chanakya and Chandragupta sit down on some rocks at the left side of the stage and start talking.]

Chandragupta: It was a very humiliating defeat, *Acharya*.

Chanakya: Yes, the battle went the wrong way for us. We were outnumbered from the very beginning.

Chandragupta: It's not just the numbers. We tried our very best and there was a point when I thought that we might win, but they are too strong. Too strong. This is happening too often, *Acharya*.

Chanakya: I know that we do not have a very large army, but we have trained our soldiers well. They are loyal to us and are fighting well. It is just that we are outnumbered each time.

Chandragupta: Who can win against the might of the Nanda empire? I think we will lose again. And again. And again. Till I die and you become old with your dream of taking revenge on King Dhana Nanda left incomplete.

Chanakya: I have been your teacher since you were seven years old, Chandra. I know you better than you know yourself. You are doing well. Do not be discouraged by temporary setbacks.

Chandragupta: I am losing hope, Acharya. We have lost too many times against the Nanda armies. I feel that failure is my destiny in life.

Chanakya: Trust me, Chandra, the Nanda armies have been lucky. They are good, but they are not invincible. They can and they will be defeated by us.

Chandragupta: When, *Acharya*, when?

Chanakya: Soon, Chandra… soon.

[The old woman comes out of the hut with her grandson. Both are carrying a plate of gruel each.]

Old woman: Sires, please do give me the opportunity of serving you. Please share our simple meal with us. It is only gruel but it is all we have, and you are welcome to share it with us.

Chandragupta: Thank you, Mother, but we cannot take anything from you. All we wanted was water and a little rest. We are ready to move on now.

Old woman: You have called me 'Mother'. No mother will allow her son to leave her home without giving him food. We are very poor and all I have is some rice gruel, but I give it with my blessing. Please take it. And you, Sire, are a learned teacher. To serve you is akin to serving the gods. Please accept this humble offering and my good wishes for all that you do.

humiliating: embarrassing, making you feel ashamed
Acharya: a Sanskrit and Hindi word for *teacher*
outnumbered: (here) the enemy was greater in number
setbacks: something that happens that delays or reverses your progress
destiny: fate, the force that some people believe controls everything that happens in a person's life
invincible: someone who cannot be defeated
gruel: a thin porridge made by boiling cereals in water or milk
akin to: similar to (something) in some way

[Both Chandragupta and Chanakya bow to her and take the plates. They sit down and wait for the steaming hot gruel to cool down. The old woman goes inside the hut and comes back with another plate of food for her grandson. The little boy immediately tries to eat the gruel from the centre of the plate and burns his fingers. He wince*s and begins to suck his burnt fingers. The old woman scolds her grandson.]*

Old woman: Hari, how many times have I told you to eat from the outer edges first. Why don't you listen to me?

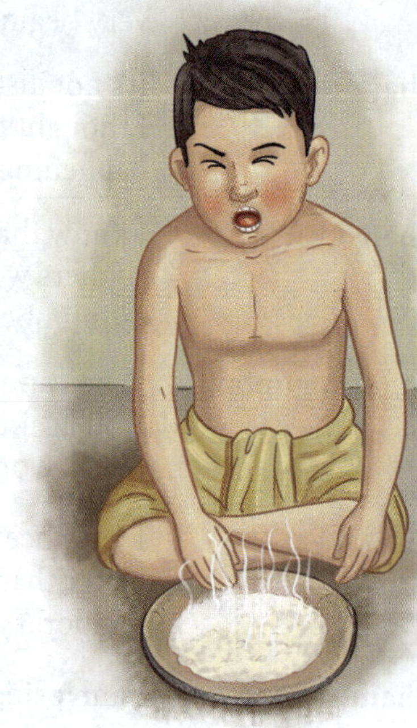

Hari: I know! You told me many times, Grandma, but I keep forgetting. Why should I eat from the outer edges first? Why is the food in the centre so hot?

Old woman: All the heat gets into the middle, and so the outer edges start cooling first. The heat in the center is very strong and will not cool quickly. That's why the outer edges start cooling quickly. Always remember this lesson son, the food in the center will be the hottest, and the food at the outer edges will be the coolest.

Chanakya: *[puts his plate down and claps for the old woman]* Mother, you are truly a wise woman. I salute you. I thank you and bow to you in gratitude, for on this day you have taught us a very valuable lesson indeed. Thank you, Mother.

Old woman: You are a teacher and a holy man, and I am a foolish old woman living in a leaking hut. Why do you mock me so, Sire? What can I, a poor old woman, teach you?

Chanakya: You do not know the worth of your own words, but I have learnt a valuable lesson from you this day, O Mother. *[turning to Chandragupta]* Chandra, listen carefully.

Chandragupta: *[astonished at the goings-on]* Yes, *Acharya*.

Chanakya: Chandra, we have been quite foolish. We have been attacking the main Nanda army, taking them head-on.

Chandragupta: And losing!

Chanakya: Yes! But that's because we have been fighting the main army which comprises the best soldiers, the greatest weapons, and the finest war elephants. Remember what this old woman said—the heat is less at the outer edges.

Chandragupta: I can't understand what you are trying to explain to me, *Acharya*.

wince**s:** suddenly makes an expression with the face that shows one is experiencing pain
gratitude: the state of feeling grateful, thankfulness
mock: make fun of
worth: value
head-on: (here) directly, face-to-face
comprises: consists of; made up of

Chanakya: It's based on what the old woman has taught us, Chandra. We will now change our strategy. We must adopt new tactics.

Chandragupta: What are these new tactics, *Acharya*? We have already been defeated too many times now.

Chanakya: That is true. But we are going to change our methods now. We shall attack suddenly without any warning and we shall attack the outer fringes of the Nanda army. They are the weakest sections with the least weapons and the worst soldiers. We attack and then we withdraw just as suddenly as we came.

Chandragupta: But how will that help us?

Chanakya: We shall not take on the whole army. We will attack at the weakest points. We shall take over small villages and forts and then slowly as our victories increase, we shall have more resources and men, and then we move in for the kill.

Chandragupta: It all seems far-fetched, *Acharya*. At the moment, I feel very demoralised.

Chanakya: No, Chandra. Failure is never the end. It is only the beginning of a new phase, a different direction, a stronger effort. Remember what they say, failure is the stepping stone to success. You are meant for great things, Chandra. Rise and keep fighting with renewed vigour and hope.

Chandragupta: Your word is my command, *Acharya*. I have obeyed you implicitly in all that I did till now, and now too you have my word that I will do everything you want me to do, with all my heart. But do you think this new method will work?

Chanakya: I am convinced that if we adopt these guerrilla warfare methods, we will surely succeed. Let us attack the outer edges of the Nanda armies.

Chandragupta: Alright, *Acharya*. I believe you. I shall not give up till we dethrone Dhana Nanda and you avenge the insults you suffered at his hands. And, on that day I promise you that you will bind up your hair. We shall carve out a kingdom that will be known all over the world.

Looking Back

Chanakya was the political and economic advisor to Chandragupta Maurya and his son Bindusara during the fourth century BC. Chanakya played an important role in grooming Chandragupta and helping him set up the Mauryan Empire. He wrote *Arthashastra*, one of the first books on political science and economics in ancient India.

strategy: a plan of action to achieve success
tactics: planned way of doing something, especially the organisation and use of soldiers and weapons in a war
fringes: the outer or less important part of an area or group
far-fetched: unlikely to be true or practical
demoralised: lost all hope and confidence; disheartened
vigour: strength, energy, and enthusiasm
implicitly: absolutely
guerrilla warfare methods: a type of war technique which uses unusual stealth methods to get results
dethrone: remove a king from his position of power
avenge: to get revenge for (something)

Looking Back

- Chandragupta Maurya was only 20 years old when he founded the Mauryan Empire. It is believed that his army had 6,00,000 foot soldiers.
- The Mauryan king voluntarily gave up his throne, handed the responsibility of the empire to his heir and son Samrat Bindusara, became a follower of Jainism, and turned into an ascetic.

Chanakya: Wellspoken, Chandra. A great destiny awaits you. Grasp it with both hands and make it a reality. Come, Chandra, let us go; Bharat awaits you.

Chandragupta: One moment, *Acharya*. I wish to do something for the old woman who has given us this priceless lesson in life before I go.

Chanakya: What is that, Chandra?

Chandragupta: With your permission, *Acharya*, I want to repair her leaking hut. She has no one to help her, and she has given us so much. Please let me repair the old mother's hut.

Chanakya: A wonderful thought, Chandra. A king must always take care of his subjects even if he is in exile. Let us help the old mother. After all, she has given us a *mantra* for success!

[Chandragupta, using the tactics he learnt from the old woman, went on to win battle after battle till he dethroned Dhana Nanda and was crowned the emperor of the Mauryan Empire.]

exile: prolonged and enforced absence from one's own home or country

mantra: (here) a word or phrase that expresses a strong belief; a motto or slogan

SUMMARY

Chandragupta, a future king and his teacher Chanakya, get tired after losing a long battle and approach an old thatched hut. They ask the old lady in the hut if they could rest there for a while. Once they settle down, they start discussing and analysing the reasons behind the lost battle. The future king has almost lost all hope after facing repeated defeats at the hands of the Nanda army. Chanakya, however, encourages him by calling such defeats as temporary setbacks. Soon after, the old lady offers them some gruel to eat. Her grandson, who is sitting nearby, tries to eat the gruel from the centre and ends up burning his fingers. Seeing this, the lady reminds the little boy to eat from the outer edges as the heat in the centre is always intense. On hearing this piece of advice, Chanakya thanks and bows to the old lady for the valuable lesson she has taught them. From then on, they use this technique for all their future battles, and go on to win each of them.

COMPREHENSION

A. Who said these words and to whom?

1. We are thirsty.
2. We were outnumbered from the very beginning.
3. Why don't you listen to me?
4. I feel that failure is my destiny in life.
5. I thank you and bow to you in gratitude, for on this day you have taught us a very valuable lesson indeed.

B. Answer these questions briefly.

1. Why did Chandragupta and Chanakya stop at the old woman's hut?
2. According to Chanakya, why were they losing the battle each time?
3. What happened when Hari tried to eat his meal of rice gruel?
4. Why did the old woman tell Hari to eat his food from the outer edges first?
5. What was the new battle strategy planned by Chanakya, based on the words of the old woman?

C. Think and answer the questions.

1. Comment on the relationship between Chandragupta and Chanakya. Did Chandragupta always listen to his teacher? Was he inspired by the wisdom of his teacher?
2. Who do you think was headstrong—Chanakya or Chandragupta? Give reasons for your answer.
3. What did Chandragupta want to do for the old woman before they left? What does this tell you about his character?

Life Skills and Values — **Learning from failure**

The child in the story burned his hands while eating the hot gruel from the centre of the plate. He made a mistake. However, he learned from the mistake to eat from the edge of the plate towards the centre. Chandragupta and Chanakya made many failed attempts at battle, till a new strategy was discovered from the old woman's lesson to the child.

Look at the various situations in school and at home where you may have made mistakes. See now, what you learned from them. How does this make you feel about trying something new or what you have labelled as 'I can't do'?

VOCABULARY

A. Match the columns to complete the proverbs. Then make sentences using any three of them.

Column A	Column B
1. Look	a. over spilt milk.
2. Don't cry	b. before you leap.
3. Never judge	c. louder than words.
4. Actions speak	d. before they hatch.
5. Don't count your eggs	e. a book by its cover.

B. Make sentences using the same word as different parts of speech.

1. a. book (as a noun)
   b. book (as a verb)
2. a. close (as an adjective)
   b. close (as a verb)
3. a. plant (as a noun)
   b. plant (as a verb)
4. a. watch (as a noun)
   b. watch (as a verb)

-able and *-ible*

- The suffix ***-able*** is used with complete root words. For example:

  enjoyable *readable* *washable*

- The suffix ***-ible*** is used with incomplete root words. For example:

  flexible *horrible* *responsible*

C. Fill in the blanks with either *-able* or *-ible* to complete the words.

1. The bed was very comfort ....
2. I had a terr .... nightmare last night.
3. My elder sister takes sens .... decisions.
4. Yesterday, I read an article about an invis .... man.
5. We asked the shopkeeper to be reason .... about the price of the pen.

GRAMMAR

Future tense

- **Future tense** is used to talk about an action that is yet to happen. For example:

  We will now change our strategy. We will attack at the weakest points.

- The simple future tense can be expressed by
  - using the simple present tense. For example:

    My vacation begins on 23 March.
  - using present continuous tense. For example:

    I am leaving for Goa tomorrow.
  - using *am/is/are going* + infinitive. For example:

    She is going to attend the meeting.

A. Complete the sentences in future tense using the correct form of words in the box.

eat	*give*	*go*	*land*	*start*	*submit*

1. We .... for a holiday next year.
2. I .... my project on Sunday.
3. The areoplane .... at 5:30 a.m.

4. We .... dinner after two hours.
5. The meeting .... in an hour from now.
6. My parents .... me a watch on my birthday.

Direct and Indirect speech

- There are two ways to report the words spoken by a person—direct or indirect speech.

Direct speech

- When the actual words of the speaker are quoted, it is called **direct speech**.
- The actual words are written within inverted commas. For example:

  The old woman said, 'My hut is old and leaking, but it is yours.'

  Chandragupta Maurya said, 'I think we will lose again.'

Indirect speech

- An **indirect speech** tells you what someone said but does not use the actual words of the speaker.
- There is no use of inverted commas. The word *that* introduces the words of the speaker. For example:

  The old woman said that her hut was old and leaking but it was theirs.

  Chandragupta Maurya said that he thought that they would lose again.

Reporting verb

If the **reporting verb** is in the past tense, the tense of the verb in the reported speech changes into one of the forms of past tense. For example:

- simple present becomes simple past:

  *Maya said, 'I **am** fine.' → Maya said that she **was** fine.*
- present continuous becomes past continuous:

  *Ruhi said, 'I **am reading**.' → Ruhi said that she **was reading**.*
- present perfect becomes past perfect:

  *Zoya said, 'I **have finished**.' → Zoya said that she **had finished**.*
- simple past becomes past perfect:

  *Zain said, 'My dog **died** last evening.'→ Zain said that his dog **had died** last evening.*

B. Change these sentences into indirect speech.

1. Anu said, 'I can paint a picture.'
2. Mohit said, 'I am feeling unwell.'
3. The young man asked, 'Where do you live?'
4. My father said, 'I am reading the newspaper.'

5. The boy said, 'I played cricket with my friends in the morning.'
6. 'I have been to Arunachal Pradesh and Nagaland,' Nibedita said.
7. Sudarshan said, 'My grandparents arrived from Madurai last Friday.'
8. Soham said to his friend, 'I have watched the programme several times.'

LISTENING AND SPEAKING

Listening

A. Listen to the passage and choose the correct answer.

1. Our elders love us .... *(periodically/unconditionally)*.
2. They help us to nurture strong .... *(materialistic/moral)* values.
3. Our elders help us to become .... *(good/selfish)* human beings.
4. We can always count on their .... *(advice/bad counsel)*.
5. We must always show our .... *(respect/love)* for our elders.

Speaking

B. Work in pairs. Role play a conversation between the old woman and a villager about her experience of meeting Chandragupta and Chanakya. You can talk about these points in your conversation.

- Sudden meeting with two great leaders
- Express your emotions or/feelings—anxious, nervous, excited
- Offering of food and accommodation
- Humility of her guests
- Advice given to grandson—inspires a new war strategy
- How she got rewarded for her hospitality and advice

WRITING

Imagine you are Chandragupta Maurya. Write a letter to your friend in the palace describing your interaction with the old woman. Your letter must cover these points.

- Where did you meet the old woman?
- Why did you stop at her hut?
- Who did she live with?
- How did she treat you?
- What did you learn from your interaction with her?
- How did you repay her kindness?
- What were your feelings or emotions?

PROJECT 3

21st Century Skills
Critical Thinking

Clean India Mission

Cleanliness is next to Godliness

India has a rich cultural heritage and a large number of historical monuments. They hold great significance and are associated with the nation's history and identity. However, people underestimate their value, and do not take good care of them. They cause an irreparable damage to them when they scribble on the walls and deface them. Also, when they do not dispose the garbage properly, they generate an unhygienic environment around the monuments.

We should take responsibility to keep the monuments clean and preserve the splendour of our heritage. Can you think of ways to improve the condition of such monuments?

Every city in India is in need of a clean-up drive. We face many problems, including open defecation, littering, spitting, and inefficient waste management. The Government of India started *Swachh Bharat Abhiyan* to address this problem. It not only seeks cooperation from the Indian citizens to keep their surroundings clean but also urges them to join hands in making the environment healthier by planting more trees. So, let's join hands and be a part of this important mission.

Interview 15 people and conduct a survey in your locality. Based on their responses, form a group and work towards improving the cleanliness in your locality.

Here's a sample questionnaire you can use for the interview. You can add your own questions to it, too.

Unleash your creativity and pen down some innovative ideas to make your locality cleaner and healthier. Write down your plan and how you would work towards achieving your goal.

Then share your experience with the class.

QUESTIONNAIRE

1. How clean is your local environment?
   Very clean   Needs improvement   Very unclean
2. Are there separate dustbins in your locality for disposing different kinds of waste?
   Yes   No
3. Which of these diseases are spread by not maintaining cleanliness and hygiene?
   Malaria   Cholera   Dengue
4. Do the government authorities visit your locality often?
   Yes   No
5. What do you think is lacking in your locality to make it an ideal place to live?
   Unclean environment   Poor sanitation   Solid waste pollution
6. What, according to you, are the ways to ensure cleanliness in your locality?
   ____
   ____
   ____
7. How will you contribute in making your locality better?
   ____
   ____
   ____

Assessment Paper

Text A

Read the article below and answer the questions that follow.

Kartik Sawhney suffered an illness shortly after his birth that left him permanently blind. However, his parents inspired in him a love of learning. Kartik's mother helped him to translate schoolwork and textbooks into braille, and Kartik learned to think of himself not as a blind boy, but as a student.

When it was time for Kartik to choose a career, the choice was not difficult. He wanted to study science and engineering. But when he expressed his desire to pursue science, he faced many obstacles. Right through his education, Kartik succeeded by adapting the rigid curriculum to his own needs.

The administrators at one of India's most prestigious institute of technology insisted that Kartik would have to take the entrance exam without the help of technology. He was disappointed. In 2013, he applied to several other schools. He got a scholarship to attend his top choice, Stanford University, and study computer science with a focus on artificial intelligence and human computer interaction.

Questions

1. When did Kartik suffer an illness? (1 mark)
2. What was the effect of the illness on him? (1 mark)
3. Who helped Kartik to study and how? (2 marks)
4. What problem did Kartik face at the entrance exam of one of India's most prestigious institute of technology? (2 marks)
5. What did Kartik study at Stanford University? (2 marks)
6. What did Kartik think of himself as? (1 mark)
7. *But when he expressed his desire to pursue science, he faced many obstacles.*

   What does 'obstacles' mean in this sentence?

   Select and copy one correct answer from:

   hurdles remarks favours points (1 mark)
8. According to you, which two qualities helped Kartik to achieve his dreams? (2 marks)

(Total marks 12)

Assessment Paper

Text B

Read the story below and answer the questions that follow.

The Baker's Dozen

Van Amsterdam was an honest baker. His Saint Nicholas* cookies, made of gingerbread, iced in red and white, were famous. One Saint Nicholas Day, an old woman asked him for a dozen cookies. When Van Amsterdam took twelve cookies and packed them, she said, 'Give me one more.' He refused. She said, 'However honest you may be, your heart is small, and your fist is tight. *Fall again, mount again, learn how to count again!*'

After that, everything started going wrong and the baker lost all his customers one by one. A year later, on the eve of Saint Nicholas Day, Van dreamed of Saint Nicholas giving him a cookie!

The next morning, the same old woman walked into the bakery and asked for a dozen cookies. This time the baker gave her thirteen cookies. 'You will surely be rewarded,' she said. When people heard Van Amsterdam counted thirteen as a dozen, he had more customers than ever. This made him extremely wealthy and popular.

* the saint who helped the needy and became known all over the world as Santa Claus

Questions

1. What was Van Amsterdam's bakery famous for? (1 mark)
2. How many cookies did the old woman ask for? (1 mark)
3. Why did Van Amsterdam disagree with the woman? (2 marks)
4. What did the woman say as she left the store the first time? (2 marks)
5. What happened after the woman left the store? (2 marks)
6. What did Saint Nicholas give Van Amsterdam in his dream? (1 mark)
7. *Fall again, mount again...*

   What does 'mount' mean in this sentence? (1 mark)

   mountain run go up sleep
8. How did Van Amsterdam become wealthy and popular? (2 marks)

(Total marks 12)